A History of the English Baptists

Volume 1

General Editor: B.R. White

D1614895

THE ENGLISH BAPTISTS OF THE SEVENTEENTH CENTURY

B. R. White

Principal, Regent's Park College

The Baptist Historical Society

This is the first volume in a new series on the English Baptists originally planned under the editorship of the late Dr E. A. Payne and now edited by Dr B. R. White.

Titles in preparation are

THE ENGLISH BAPTISTS OF THE EIGHTEENTH CENTURY

by Raymond Brown

THE ENGLISH BAPTISTS OF THE NINETEENTH CENTURY

by J. H. Y. Briggs

Cover design by Jo Crabbe

1983

The Baptist Historical Society
4 Southampton Row, London, WC1B 4AB

ISBN 0 903166 07 0

All rights reserved. No part of this publication may be reproduced, stored in a retrieval system, or transmitted in any form or by any means, electronic, mechanical, photo-copying, recording or otherwise, without the prior permission of the Baptist Historical Society.

CONTENTS

WILLIAM KIFFIN

AN INTRODUCTION TO ENGLISH BAPTIST HISTORY

Denominational history is more than a little unfashionable today. For this there at first seem good reasons. To the ecumenically minded it appears uncomfortably like the rehearsal of the battle cries and the occasional battle scars of a yesterday which would be better forgotten. To the historian, especially to the professional historian, denominational history seems too much like cardboard, a dry and flat narrative dissociated from the flesh and blood of political, economic, social and intellectual history which has been written up by amateur antiquarians arguing about irrelevant sectarian family trees. In addition, the Baptist story, perhaps especially, is too often thought to be characterized by a fragmentation, a seeming dissidence of dissent, which makes its seventeenth century record an especially rockstrewn and unprofitable subject for serious historical enquiry.

Yet, especially for the ecumenically committed, it is useful to clarify the tradition and to establish the identity and inner drives and characteristics of one significant group of Christian churches. A great deal of nonsense has been talked by Baptists, among others, in ecumenical discussions because the roots of their tradition have not been carefully uncovered and studied. For the historian also, especially if concerned to understand those generations of Englishmen when religion was the passionate concern of many of his fellow-countrymen, there may be gain in the portraiture, albeit in the bold strokes of near caricature, of the English Baptists in the light of the last generation's researches. So, although this first part of the history will need to by-pass many of the wider questions its own narrative provokes, it will attempt to outline the early development of the English Baptists and the characteristic convictions which informed their life together and the structures which provided its framework.

For Baptists themselves a knowledge of their tradition may inform the decisions which they must take today which will shape their tomorrow. Many Baptists have been unclear about what is of primary and what is of secondary importance to their continuing testimony: for example, some have considered that the conviction that baptism should be by immersion is almost as important as the conviction that it should be administered to believers; others have believed that the Baptist church meeting was intended to be like a gathering of shareholders rather than an occasion where the will of God was sought and obeyed.

To understand that continuing testimony and to evaluate it requires studies in some depth: it would not be adequate merely to obtain a record of things done, decisions taken, assertions made and institutions created without some explanation of the reasons for them. Such studies could enable Baptists not only to understand why in earlier days they said and did what they did but also could enable them to explain themselves more adequately to other Christians. A clearer view of their own story could also enable them to see their own present situation in perspective and so help them to see whether their arguments and precedents from the past could still be fruitful today.

The re-creation of their denominational past has been useful for Baptists in the present in three other ways. First, it has reminded them of certain standards of commitment and devotion which were in danger of being forgotten or of being too easily brushed aside. Secondly, it has shown something of how often past policies and insights were shaped by accident, ignorance and, sometimes, selfishness as well as by prudence, wisdom and costly sacrifice, and so has warned against being too unconditionally committed to the policies and insights of the present. Thirdly, it has helped men and women to see that neither their own policies and insights nor those of any one section of the Church were or are the whole story of God's dealings with his people across the years.

Tradition, even for those Baptists who normally and hastily deny any importance or authority to such a concept, means the living stream of their denominational yesterday in the lives of individuals, in their writings, in their congregations and in those other institutions in which the Spirit has been continually at work striving with them and against them across the years.

Baptist Definitions and Assumptions

It is necessary to emphasize first that, from their separate beginnings down to 1891, the larger number of Baptists of England formed not one community but two. The older group, the General Baptists, gained their name because they believed, with the followers of the Dutch theologian Jacobus Arminius, that Christ died for all men. They therefore believed in "general redemption" from their first beginnings in the exiled congregation in Amsterdam of John Smyth and Thomas Helwys. The younger group, the Particular or Calvinistic Baptists, who seem to have arisen among the underground congregations of London in the 1630s, believed that Christ died only for the elect.

Both groups shared a very similar position on many aspects of the doctrine of the Church. For example, they both believed that the visible church of Christ was composed of gathered congregations of believing men and women and they both believed in and practised (at least from 1642) believer's baptism by immersion. Nevertheless, they consistently organized separately, differed in their views of inter-congregational relationships and the ministry and, on the whole, flourished in different parts of the country. Normally too, though some General Baptist congregations, such as those at Reading and Coventry, and some General Baptist individuals, such as Benjamin Keach and Mark Key, became Particular Baptists, there was little movement in the reverse direction. A much smaller group, the Seventh Day Baptists, were usually though not invariably Calvinist in their theology, and first seem to have developed during the 1650s. They seem only to have differed from the larger Baptist groups in their conviction that the Seventh Day was divinely ordained as much for Christian as for Jewish worship. Several generations of the Stennett family were their most notable contribution to the ongoing English Baptist tradition.

The Calvinistic or Particular Baptists stood close to the clear-cut Calvinism of the seventeenth century Independents (as the Congregationalists were then most often known). The Particular Baptist Confession of 1644 was largely indebted to the Separatist Confession of 1596 with its Calvinism stiffened by the teaching of William Ames (an early Independent) and probably the Council of Dort. Similarly, the most influential of all the Calvinistic Baptist confessions of faith was that first accepted in 1677 and re-published at the Particular Baptist London Assembly of 1689. This was, in fact, a Baptist modification of the Independents' Savoy Confession (1658) which was in its turn a modification of the Presbyterian Westminster Confession (1647).

The close agreement of much of the theology and ecclesiology of the Calvinistic Baptists and the Independents helps to explain another difference between the Generals and the Particulars. While the General Baptists all seem to have remained consistently 'closed membership', that is, they would allow no-one to join their churches unless he had been baptized as a believer, the Calvinistic Baptists during the seventeenth century and afterwards were divided on the matter. It is clear that from their early days of expansion in the 1640s and 1650s most Calvinistic Baptists practised 'closed membership' and, almost certainly as an invariable corollary, 'closed communion', that is, they would allow no-one to share the Lord's Supper with them unless he had been baptized as a believer. Nevertheless, from those early days, there were Independent churches which tolerated the practice of both forms of baptism - of infants and of believers - and there were churches which were or became predominantly Baptist which continued to include members who had only been baptized as infants. John Bunyan's church at Bedford seems to have been one of the former and the churches of John Tombs and Henry Jessey appear to have been examples of the latter. The originally Independent congregation meeting in Broadmead, Bristol, was an early example of one which moved from being predominantly Independent to being predominantly Baptist. Such congregations, of course, practised 'open communion'. During the 1650s and, intermittently, for long afterwards many 'closed membership' leaders and their churches were sharply critical of those who practised 'open membership' alleging that they were behaving in a disorderly fashion. A misplaced charity, it was suggested, had triumphed over a proper concern for true, scriptural, order. Nevertheless, some of the bitterness seems to have died away during the Great Persecution and, by the time the London Assembly of 1689 was summoned, it had evidently been agreed that Broadmead, for example, should be invited to join the meeting of largely 'closed membership' churches.

Unfortunately the considerable fame of the Broadmead Records and that of John Tombs, Henry Jessey and John Bunyan (whom many Baptists like to claim as their own) has led to a serious distortion in the writing of the early history of the Particular Baptists: those with 'open membership' convictions have been taken by historians not only as the norm but as therefore an integral part of the early Calvinistic Baptist body. Yet the fact is that the 'open membership' churches were in a minority and that those who organized the nationwide Particular Baptist network of associations in the 1650s were all convinced of 'closed membership'. Of course, this is not to deny friendships between those holding the different positions but it does mean that they did not, in this early period, have what is technically known as 'church fellowship', that is, they did not co-operate together in a common life and mission.

These divisions among Baptists with their concerns over what may now seem mere footnotes to ecclesiology, can only be understood if certain of their implicit assumptions are made clear. These assumptions, essentially about the authority of the Bible for matters of church order, underlay all early Baptist thinking about the nature of the Church and, to a very great degree, still influence the thinking - and the feelings - of many Baptists all over the world in the twentieth century also.

Although these were axiomatic for early Baptist thinking they could not easily be proved from Scripture, but it is easy to see how they led to a profound concern for the right interpretation of Scripture. Furthermore, during the seventeenth century and for nearly two centuries afterwards, these assumptions were frequently unquestioned since they were often shared by many of their Protestant rivals.

Basically, it was assumed that the Bible was not only the final authority on earth for matters such as Christology and the Atonement but also that it provided the final and authoritative teaching for all necessary matters concerned with the true nature and constitution of the Church. On this assumption a number of others were built: it was assumed that in the apostolic age the Church was organised and constituted according to one pattern only and that the New Testament provided enough evidence of that pattern to enable those who came after to reconstruct it. But this was not merely an academic matter: with it there went the assumption that the one pattern could be and must be reconstituted by any later generation of Christians even in a situation of total apostasy. The one pattern, as the Anabaptists had believed in the age of the Reformation and as the English Separatists were to believe during the age of Elizabeth I, demanded that the church comprise not everyone in the parish but a committed, convinced and converted group of believing men and women. When they saw this truth the group had the right and duty to form themselves into a church under the guidance of the Risen Christ. Furthermore, they possessed his power to accept other members into fellowship with them and had the duty to discipline and even, if necessary, to cast out those who erred either in doctrine or in conduct. At the same time such a congregation ultimately had also the power to elect or dismiss its officers even if there were no other Christian group able to share the responsibility with them.

An obvious consequence of all this was that it was held to be a betrayal of the fellowship if, after the one true apostolic pattern for the church had been reconstructed and reconstituted, any members should have further dealings with a false church such as the Church of England which had gained its essential constitution (and its baptism!) not from the Bible but from the apostate Church of Rome. It was, of course, also believed that, once the true pattern had been reconstructed it could and must be reconstituted as a matter of urgent obedience to Christ in any place, at any time, by any people who had grasped its truth. Not to do so was to fail in a prime requirement of biblical, and therefore of Christian, discipleship. This concern for the reconstitution of the apostolic model explains why, in so many Baptist documents, the argument was not considered complete without Scripture references. In all their arguments, debates, struggles, they were trying to discover what was the will of God and then to bring their practice, whether about baptism, church membership, the laying on of hands, the payment of tithes, the ministry, their duty to the state or anything else into conformity with that will.

So, while they were prepared to allow that they had not yet perfectly seen, nor perfectly obeyed every detail of the divine pattern they naturally required that their critics should give clear and adequate evidence from Scripture for <u>their</u> position before expecting the Baptists to move from the ground they already occupied. A certain humility because of their sense that the Lord had yet more light and truth to break forth out of his written Word is embodied in a classic form in the 1646 edition of the London Particular Baptist *Confession*:

> Also we confess that we now know but in part and that we are ignorant of many things which we desire and seek to know: and if any shall do us that friendly part to show us from the Word of God that we see not, we shall have cause to be thankful to God and to them.

<u>Historians of the English Baptists</u>

From the first, Baptist historians in England have not merely tried to give as adequate a narrative as their sources allow but have seen their task as that of defending their co-religionists and of influencing denominational policy.

This can be seen even in the work of Thomas Crosby (?1685-1752). Crosby was a stubborn, quarrelsome, mathematician and schoolmaster in Southwark who was the first Baptist historian to publish a completed work, *The History of the English Baptists* (4 vols., 1738-40). He was son-in-law to Benjamin Keach (1640-1704) and was a church member at

Horslydown, Southwark during the pastorate of Keach's other son-in-law and successor as minister, Benjamin Stinton (1676-1719). Stinton had himself made considerable progress in collecting material for a history of his own but the project was postponed by his unexpected and early death. Crosby, who seems to have been devoted to Stinton, preserved his manuscripts but, for several years, did little with them. He then offered them to Daniel Neale for use in the latter's projected *History of the Puritans* which was eventually published in 1732. To Crosby's angry disgust Neale passed over the Baptists' share in the story with rather less than five unsympathetic pages. Crosby's reaction was to determine to publish a history of the Baptists himself.

Apart from attempting a narrative history Crosby sought to put the Baptist case from three particular points of view. First, he attempted to prove the rightness of believer's baptism by citing a variety of arguments, biblical, theological and historical, in its support. Secondly, he tried firmly to dissociate the English Baptists from the continental Anabaptists especially, of course, those involved in the tragedy of Munster in 1534-35. Thirdly, by providing biographical sketches of early Baptist leaders, he attempted to prove his assertion that 'men of the greatest learning and piety have neither been ashamed nor afraid in the worst of times to stand up in vindication of a principle so truly apostolic (believer's baptism) though ever so much despised and hated'. In short, it was his intention, as he himself explicitly affirmed, 'to remove, or prevent, or allay scandal or censure for time to come'.

He was also greatly concerned about the doctrinal divisions which separated the General Baptists from the Particular Baptists at the time he wrote, for he believed they should not exist. Indeed, he insisted 'I am fully persuaded and clearly of opinion that this difference in opinion is not a sufficient or reasonable ground of renouncing Christian communion with one another, and therefore have not, in the course of this history, leaned either to one side or to the other, but have taken facts as they have come to my hands, without regarding to which of the parties they were peculiar'. There can be little doubt that this view had been held by Benjamin Stinton and may have been inherited by Crosby from him.

Since Crosby's work is neither systematic nor analytical it is important to note that it is largely based on manuscripts and printed works which are still available to the historian. Only, therefore, in occasional instances, for example, as in the anecdote about William Kiffin's gift to Charles II, does he preserve material not otherwise accessible from the period before Stinton's death. However, during the years after 1719, he provides some interesting information of his own and some not disinterested criticism of the London Particular Baptist ministers whom he knew.

It is a little surprising that the Baptists, of all the Dissenters, appear to have been first in the field with a denominational history, for the Quakers kept better records and the Congregationalists and Presbyterians certainly produced more famous leaders and scholars. Why then was Benjamin Stinton, as early as 1711, beginning to gather materials for a history? There are two possible explanations. First, the last years of Queen Anne were a time of growing pressure upon the Dissenters generally and the Baptists were still regarded as less respectable than either the Presbyterians or the Congregationalists and probably as potentially more dangerous, as a possible group of revolutionaries, than the Quakers. Stinton may well have felt that a history, which had been projected earlier, would be one way of showing that Baptists were, generally, a peaceable people. Secondly, when the pressure was relieved by the accession of George I, Stinton still continued with his historical records and left plenty of evidence of his own concern to draw the General and Particular Baptists together. His activity was not merely limited to argument or writing: it was evidently he who was the prime mover in launching a united London fraternal of Baptist ministers. It seems likely, therefore, that the original scheme of a denominational history was launched both as an exercise in apologetics and nurtured, also, by a concern for uniting the Baptists.

While Thomas Crosby's work was done at a time when the older Dissent, including the Baptists, was declining both in confidence and in numbers the second notable contribution to the writing of Baptist history was made half a century later in a very different situation. John Rippon (1751-1836) had been trained for the ministry at the reorganized Bristol Baptist Academy before becoming minister in Southwark in 1773 in succession to the high Calvinist John Gill (1699-1771) who had himself succeeded Benjamin Stinton. Rippon's lifetime saw a new confidence engendered among dissenters generally by the impact of the Evangelical Revival. His own work for Baptist history in the production of *The Baptist Register* (4 vols., 1790-1802) was done in a period of just over a decade which was to see that confidence marked by a great leap forward in missionary enthusiasm beginning with the foundation of the Baptist Missionary Society in 1792. Although he was concerned to collect and publish documents rather than to write a connected history, his work was important enough to require inclusion in company with those who actually produced narrative histories.

Rippon himself was also an advocate of the evangelical Calvinism characteristic of Andrew Fuller (1754-1815); he was active too in the support of the infant Missionary Society and, later, shared in the support of the early years of the Baptist Union. He was also immensely interested in the collection and publication of both early and contemporary Baptist documents and statistics from Britain and America. While *The Baptist Register* was to prove a valuable quarry for others the only narrative history Rippon published was *A History of the Welsh Association* (1795) by Joshua Thomas of Leominster (1719-1797). Thomas's manuscripts, chiefly but not entirely concerned with Welsh Baptist History and still largely unpublished, remain mines of information.

Joseph Ivimey (1773-1834), who was born the year Rippon arrived in Southwark and died two years before him, made the next major narrative contribution with his *History of the English Baptists* (4 vols., 1811-1830). As for many years minister of the Particular Baptist Church at Eagle Street, London, he was an active writer and theological controversialist, deeply concerned for denominational affairs and, perhaps especially, for the Baptist Irish Society. He was also able to search out and use some of the oldest London congregations' records. While, therefore, he certainly owed much to the work of Crosby and Rippon he was also able to add a good deal of material he had himself discovered as he brought the story down to 1820.

Like Crosby, Ivimey too set out to act both as the apologist for the Baptists and as their critic as well as their historian. In the first volume of his work he asserted that 'the English Baptists held the genuine principles of the Reformation and pursued them to their legitimate consequences. Believing that the Bible alone contains the religion of Protestants, they rejected everything in the worship of God which was not found in the sacred oracles'. Secondly, he attempted to show that in England infant baptism owed its origin to Popery and, thirdly, that the English Baptists 'were the first persons who understood the important doctrine of Christian liberty, and who zealously opposed all persecution for the sake of conscience'.

Since Ivimey's volumes were published with intervals of several years between each one and the next it was not surprising that changing concerns were reflected in them as the work developed. His second volume was especially dedicated, as he explained in its preface, to demonstrating the worth of those who had been ministers in the past and to awakening contemporary 'Baptist ministers and churches to imitate the piety, simplicity and zeal of their progenitors'. His third volume had, he said, as a primary concern that of answering those who thought the Baptists were 'the most sectarian of sects, the most entrenched and fortified in the narrow circle of its communion'. In the preface to his final volume, however, Ivimey turned his attention once more inwards to his own denomination: after discussing some of its strengths he rebuked some of its weaknesses. Among these he listed open communion, ignorant ministers, tyrannical deacons and, more generally, disobedience to Christ!

The only General Baptist among the early historians was Adam Taylor (1768-1833) who produced his two-volume *A History of the English General Baptists* in 1818. He was the son of a General Baptist minister and the nephew of Daniel Taylor: the leader of the New Connexion of General Baptists. A schoolmaster in London for most of his life, he was editor of the *General Baptist Repository* 1810-22 and wrote extended *Memoirs* of both his uncle and of his father. Taylor, like the New Connexion of General Baptists to which he belonged, was the product of the Evangelical Revival and he wrote quite deliberately to explain the position and to describe the origins of his people. Writing eighty years after Crosby's first volume had been published, Taylor ignored the suggestion of closer links between the General and Particular Baptists. Instead he regretted Crosby's deliberate confusion of the two groups since he believed that, as a consequence, the part played by the early General Baptists in the seventeenth century had been underestimated. Indeed, he explained that a major motive for his own work was to give the General Baptists, 'their due share in the religious transactions of the seventeenth century'. His second explicit motive in writing was to do justice to the doctrinal orthodoxy of the early General Baptists since so many of their more recent leaders had 'widely departed from the faith and doctrine of their predecessors'. This had caused the doctrinal position of the New Connexion of General Baptists, whose Christological convictions were entirely orthodox, to be widely misunderstood by other Christians. One great value of the first volume of Adam Taylor's work to later historians has continued to be its quotation from such lost records as the early Berkhamsted churchbook. Although not without criticisms of Crosby, Taylor nevertheless asserted that 'his volumes will always be valuable as a depository of facts and documents, which will continue to assist every succeeding writer'.

In his second volume Taylor dealt largely with the history of those older congregations which had united with the new body and its leaders. He stressed that he had given some account of their failures as well as of their triumphs so that such narratives of the darker side of the story should 'excite every reader, but especially every minister, to be more earnest and constant in praying for grace to preserve him from giving any occasion to the enemies of the truth to blaspheme and doubly vigilant in shunning every appearance of evil'.

During the remainder of the nineteenth century other Baptists were to produce histories of the denomination which took the story beyond the chronological limits of the classic writers already mentioned. Nevertheless, usually the later nineteenth century authors added little to the information about the seventeenth and eighteenth centuries provided by Crosby, Rippon, Ivimey and Taylor. The one notable exception in the provision of new sources was the set of publications sponsored in the middle years of the century by the 'Hanserd Knollys Society'. Not only were two volumes of rare tracts and other documents produced but two volumes of church records were also published: *The Broadmead Records* (1847) edited by Edward Bean Underhill and the records of the seventeenth century congregations at *Fenstanton, Warboys and Hexham* (1854) also edited by Underhill.

It was not, however, until W T Whitley (1861-1947) that English Baptist history began to be studied in any systematic way and by modern methods. Whitley worked for forty years in the Baptist ministry in England, Australia and then at home in England again. He was not only a very careful pastor but took part in denominational affairs as well as all kinds of historical investigations. He led in the formation of the Baptist Historical Society (1908) and became the first editor and for many years the most prolific contributor to the Society's *Transactions* (1908-1921) and its successor, the *Baptist Quarterly*. But his services to Baptist history extended also into other fields: he edited and published the *Minutes of the General Assembly of the General Baptists 1654-1811* (2 vols., 1907, 1910), the *Amersham and Ford Churchbooks* (1912), the *Works of John Smyth* (2 vols., 1915) and the *Baptist Bibliography* (2 vols., 1916, 1922). In 1923 he published his *History of British Baptists* (rev. edn. 1932) which provides the first substantial modern account of their history.

The most recent comprehensive study, by A C Underwood, *The History of the English Baptists* (1947) benefited greatly from Whitley's work and provided a readable replacement for his *History*. Underwood's book made the first attempt to use the insights provided by the sociology of religion but probably gave too much attention to John Smyth's part in Baptist beginnings - perhaps because of the ready availability of Smyth's Works. It is significant that, consciously or unconsciously, Underwood, like his predecessors, also hoped to tell a plain tale plainly, together with a defence and explanation of the Baptist case and an attempt to mould the thinking, perhaps the policy, of the denomination. There can be little doubt in the mind of anyone reading the later pages of his book that the principal, as he then was, of Rawdon Baptist College in Yorkshire intended on the one hand to support a conservative attitude on such matters as those of reunion and the autonomy of individual congregations and, on the other, to encourage a re-thinking of the theology of baptism.

During the last thirty years the writings of Dr E A Payne have pointed the way for a younger generation of Baptist historians. His local history, *The Baptists of Berkshire* (1951), his numerous articles in the *Baptist Quarterly* and elsewhere, together with his profound concern to keep the questions posed by the ecumenical movement before Baptist eyes have all served the cause of better Baptist history writing. While his largest book was *The Baptist Union: a Short History* (1958), which made the first considerable attempt to review many facets of English Baptist life in the period since 1810, his most influential was almost certainly *The Fellowship of Believers* (1944, rev. edn. 1952). This book was deeply concerned to stress the variety and richness of the twofold English Baptist tradition and sought to recall Baptists to their historic churchmanship as revealed by a wide variety of writings across the centuries.

Some further material on Baptist historians can be found in my articles on Thomas Crosby in the Baptist Quarterly XXI (1965-6) and on 'The task of a Baptist Historian' Baptist Quarterly XXII (1967-8). There is also a fine Oxford D.Phil thesis available in the Angus Library, Regent's Park College, by K R Manley 'John Rippon D D, 1751-1836 and the Particular Baptists' (1967).

THE ENGLISH BAPTISTS OF THE SEVENTEENTH CENTURY

1. The English General Baptists to 1660

Long before John Smyth and Thomas Helwys there had been 'Anabaptists' (that is, 're-baptizers') in England. Although Henry VIII had caught a few and burned some, most if not all of these had been foreigners. Under Edward VI a number were gaoled and forced to recant but only two, Joan of Kent and the Dutch surgeon George van Parris, were executed. But Edward's government continued to be anxious about the spread of views they termed 'Anabaptist' in south-eastern England. Some of those who dissociated themselves from the Edwardian protestant establishment seem actually to have been opposed to the practice of infant baptism but others may usually have been lay Bible students more opposed to the spread of theological ideas associated with Calvinism. Certainly it has proved difficult to develop an adequate definition of the various groups of radicals. Their most articulate and effective leader was Henry Hart who seems to have managed to remain free and active well into the reign of Queen Mary. After the accession of Elizabeth I all traces of an English radical movement which could accurately be described as in any sense 'Anabaptist' seem quickly to have disappeared although, in 1575, some Dutch Anabaptists were executed in London.[1]

Nobody doubts that the English General Baptists first evolved from the English Separatists but there is dispute as to whether the 16th century Anabaptist movement, either in England or on the continent, had any measureable influence upon the development of the Separatists.

Although, at first sight, the disappearance of the earlier English radical movement just on the eve of the appearance of the Separatists and the similarities between both concepts of the 'gathered church' suggest a link, the question of the possibility of influence is made virtually insoluble by the incontrovertible existence of three complicating factors. First, it was entirely possible for both groups to come independently to the same conclusions about the essential nature of the Christian Church because they both shared the frequent protestant tendency to appeal to the Bible as providing the one unchanging pattern or blueprint for the faith. Secondly, even if the Separatists did learn anything from the Anabaptists they were highly unlikely to admit this for two reasons: first, because they were always concerned to emphasize that their convictions were derived directly from the Bible and not from the traditions of men and, secondly, because they would know that to quote the Anabaptists as the source for any idea was a quick way in both the 16th and 17th centuries to close men's minds to its acceptance. Thirdly, there does exist, in the records of the evolution of the English Separatists, a plausible explanation of the development of their views which does not require the introduction of 'Anabaptist' influence[2].

In an article entitled 'Who were the Baptists?'[3] Dr W S Hudson suggested that certain ecumenical issues for the present day underlay the answer to his question but it may reasonably be argued that these are irrelevant both for the historian and even for the contemporary ecumenical enthusiast. No amount of theological or historical sleight of hand can make <u>either</u> of the main groups of 17th century English Baptists comfortable participants in 20th century ecumenical debate. In his reply to Dr Hudson's article Dr E A Payne effectively countered those arguments which might seem to make the idea of the influence of continental Anabaptists upon English Baptists impossible and asserted: 'The religious life of the seventeenth century was like a tumultuous sea, blown upon by winds from several directions. That one strong current of air came from the Anabaptist movement in the previous century I am convinced'.[4] It is certainly more plausible to argue for the likelihood of influence from Anabaptists upon 17th century English Baptist beginnings than it is from Anabaptism upon the earlier Separatists. Even so it should be noted that two careful articles seeking to estimate the influence of Anabaptism upon both General and Calvinistic Baptist origins found that no significant influence could be decisively proved.[5]

John Smyth, Thomas Helwys and the first General Baptists

It was John Smyth (1570-1612?) whose rhetorical question, 'is not the visible church of the New Testament with all the ordinances thereof the chief and principal part of the Gospel?' underlined what was to become the fundamental Baptist concern for the next generation and more - a concern for the right establishment of the visible church of Christ upon earth. When Smyth, Thomas Helwys and their friends escaped to exile in Amsterdam during 1608 they were certainly convinced Separatists in their churchmanship and, almost as certainly, convinced Calvinists in the general framework of their theology.

Probably three factors played a part in convincing them that Christian baptism should be for believers only. First, there was a longstanding unease of all Separatists with the baptism which they had received in what they believed to be the apostate Church of England. Secondly, there was the continuing Bible study which stemmed from their restless desire to re-model the visible church towards what they believed to be the apostolic ideal. Thirdly, there was the practice of believer's baptism by the Mennonites in Amsterdam. Their unease must have sharpened the question, their Bible study and their knowledge of Mennonite practice may well have provided an answer.

However, it seems that at that time Smyth believed the Mennonites to be in error on other doctrinal matters and therefore that he could not turn to them for baptism. Consequently, as John Robinson was later to report, 'Mr Smith baptized first himself and next Mr Helwys and so the rest'. This, it should be remembered, was not baptism by immersion but 'out of a bason', perhaps by washing the faces of those to be baptized as the earlier Separatists had done when they had baptized their children.[6]

There is no evidence in any of his extant writings of how John Smyth came at the same time to hold views later characterized by the name of the moderate Dutch Calvinist theologian Jacobus Arminius. It is possible that Smyth had pondered the somewhat similar opinions argued in Cambridge some years earlier by Peter Baro and it is certain that the Mennonites were strongly critical of scholastic Calvinism. It is also clear that no-one with any theological interest at all could avoid being aware of the controversy raging in the Netherlands at the time nor, perhaps, could one be aware of the controversy without feeling the need to choose sides.

While some might well feel that a Calvinist view of election and reprobation would better fit a church based on believer's baptism than one based on infant baptism it may have seemed to Smyth that 'Arminian' views consorted better with the responsibility laid upon individuals in believer's baptism. At all events, Richard Clifton, one of his Separatist opponents, soon reported that Smyth had circulated a paper in which he maintained two positions, '1. Christ's redemption stretcheth to all men. 2. Man hath not lost the faculty of willing any good thing that is showed him'.[7] Such views, developed and modified as the years wore on, were to be characteristic of and to justify the name of

'General' Baptists throughout their history for they believed in general redemption, that Christ died for all.

Smyth had acted very boldly both in baptizing himself and in contradicting Calvinistic orthodoxy but he came to feel, after closer acquaintance with the Mennonites, that they were not heretical and that he had therefore been wrong to reject the possibility of baptism at their hands. He had originally acted upon the assumption that he was in a situation of total Christian apostasy in which all succession in apostolic faith and practice over baptism had been broken so that, he wrote, 'there was no church to whom we could join with a good conscience to have baptism from them'. But when he had concluded that the Mennonites were not heretical and that he ought to have sought baptism from them, he discovered that Thomas Helwys held that, even if there were true churches in existence, Christians 'are not bound to join to those former churches established but may, being as yet unbaptized, baptize themselves (as we did) and proceed to build churches of themselves'.[8]

This disagreement led to a division in the church and, while Smyth and the majority of the congregation worked towards closer fellowship with the Mennonites, Helwys and a small group held aloof and wrote to the Mennonites urging that this was unnecessary. About succession in the administration of baptism they argued: 'John Baptist being unbaptized preached the baptism of repentance and they that believed and confessed their sins he baptized. And whosoever shall now be stirred up by the same Spirit, to preach the same word, and men thereby being converted, may according to John his example, wash them with water and who can forbid?'[9] Smyth's comment upon this position was that such disorderly policies would lead to there being 'as many churches as couples in the world and none have anything to do with other: which breaketh the bond of love and brotherhood in churches'.

Eventually, though John Smyth himself died of tuberculosis in 1612, the union between the majority of his followers and the Mennonites was completed in January 1615. Meanwhile Thomas Helwys and his tiny group of supporters had drawn up *A Declaration of Faith* (1611)[10] in Amsterdam which, after emphasising that 'God would have all men saved', in flat contradiction to Calvinistic orthodoxy, also provided an outline of their ecclesiological convictions. These, which were to be closely followed by later General Baptist confessions, were, as might be expected, strongly marked by the Separatist tradition out of which they had grown.

Helwys and his friends believed that 'the church of Christ is a company of faithful people ... separated from the world by the Word and Spirit of God ... being knit unto the Lord and unto one another by baptism ... upon their own confession of the faith ... and sins'. They then stressed that while in Christ the Church is one it consists of 'divers particular congregations' each of which, guided by the Bible, is immediately responsible to Christ alone. An individual congregation, they held, is complete even without officers so its members 'may and ought, when they are come together, to pray, prophesy, break bread and administer in all the holy ordinances although as yet they have no officers, or that their officers should be in prison, sick, or by any other means hindered from the church'. Such extreme statements of independency and congregational isolation necessarily reflect the extreme situation of a pioneer group under persecution. Their views were to be modified as General Baptists grew in numbers.

However, they had much more to say which was of importance for their doctrine of the Church. Every church, they believed, must receive all its members by baptism which as 'washing with water ... is ... the outward manifestation of dying unto sin ... and therefore in no wise appertaineth to infants'. No congregation should be too large for members to 'have particular knowledge one of another' for they ought to 'perform all the duties of love one towards another both to soul and body'. While the Lord's Supper is the 'outward manifestation of the spiritual communion between Christ and the faithful mutually', members guilty of sin and remaining impenitent must be excommunicated but must not be avoided 'in respect of civil society'. At the same time, since the church ought to meet each Lord's Day 'to pray, prophesy, praise God and break bread and perform all other parts of spiritual communion for the worship of God', no members should work at their worldly callings on that day.

Each church should appoint two kinds of officer: elders, who 'do especially feed the flock concerning their souls', and deacons, 'men and women who by their office relieve the necessities of the poor and impotent brethren concerning their bodies'. Such officers must be elected by 'that church or congregation whereof they are members' and have no authority outside it. Unlike the Mennonites Helwys and his friends believed that the civil government was not only 'a holy ordinance of God' but also that civil governors 'may be members of the church of Christ' and that 'it is lawful in a just cause for the deciding of strife to take an oath by the name of the Lord'.

Such were the convictions held by the group which Thomas Helwys led back to England. They apparently returned in 1612 and printed *A Short Declaration of The Mystery of Iniquity* with an appeal to King James I for toleration of both their beliefs and those of others. At the end of the book Helwys explained his conviction that it was a Christian duty not to flee from persecution and made clear that he and his people were under no illusion about the possible consequences of their return: they had come, he wrote, 'to lay down their lives in their own country for Christ and his truth'.

By 1616 Helwys was dead and for a further quarter of a century his followers could only manage to maintain a precarious, underground existence in their native country. What is known of them is largely drawn from the fragmentary correspondence which has survived in the Mennonite archives in Amsterdam together with certain illegal publications of their own.

It seems that after Helwys' death the London congregation was led by another returned exile, John Murton. In 1615 they published *Objections argued by way of dialogue ... that no man ought to be persecuted for his religion* but this had no discernible effect in easing official policy. Another work entitled *A description of what God hath predestinated* (1620) asserted their Arminian position: that baptism should follow faith as a condition of membership of a true church and that 'every disciple that hath ability is authorized, yea commanded, to preach, convert and baptize as well and as much (if not more) than a pastor'.

Over a century ago Benjamin Evans printed English versions of some letters from the Mennonite archives in Amsterdam which tell a little about the situation of the English General Baptists during the 1620s.[11]

The earliest of these letters reports a division in the London congregation. This, apparently, took place in the spring of 1624 while John Murton was still alive when Elias Tookey and fifteen others separated because Murton and the majority were insisting on certain Christological assertions with too great strictness. It appears that Tookey and his friends agreed with the others in thinking it right to swear oaths when required by the authorities and even that Christians should be prepared to fight in a 'just war'. They sought help from Amsterdam in reconciling them but what eventually happened is unknown.

A letter of 1626 makes it clear that the main London congregation and the churches associated with it at Lincoln, Sarum, Coventry and Tiverton still differed from the Mennonites over the legality of oaths and the right of church members to become magistrates. As a result, although they believed it 'becomes all of us who love the same Lord Jesus Christ and his truth to try for unity in all manners, and to walk with all and everyone, as belonging to the same society' they were quite prepared to differ from the brethren in Amsterdam. When they wrote Tookey's group still maintained a separate existence and the main body of the five congregations amounted in all to about one hundred and fifty people. They believed that in the absence of a properly appointed pastor those recognised as preachers might administer the sacraments. However, since not all the congregations included recognized preachers, it was not possible to administer the Lord's Supper every week as they wished. In 1630 another letter was sent from Amsterdam to Lincoln but it was clear that no union was possible between the English and the Dutch congregations because of their differences over relationships with the state.

While there is no certain evidence that the London church of General Baptists persisted through the difficult years of the 1630s it seems reasonable to believe that the Bell Alley congregation of the 1640s was in the direct succession of those who had returned with Thomas Helwys. Other underground congregations survived through the 1630s and the lack of evidence about this one may only be due to its success in keeping out the hands of the authorities.

The Coming of the Great Rebellion

The Long Parliament began to sit in November 1640 and soon after began to dismantle the machinery of ecclesiastical repression and the very institution of episcopacy. These and other challenges to the king's authority led to the outbreak of the Civil War in the summer of 1642. With the Civil War came the English Revolution. And revolution was the background against which Baptists of every type and other sectaries also began to develop. The smear label 'Anabaptist' which was attached to the Baptists in particular by contemporaries was itself a term guaranteed to link them with the atrocities which, as all men knew, though none knew precisely, had been committed by a violent group of Anabaptists at Munster a century before. As it was the sectaries, whatever their name, all posed a very considerable threat to the religious and political establishment with their radical appeal to the Bible against the traditions of the Church and, occasionally, with an even more radical appeal to their individual inner convictions independent of and even opposed to the Bible. The execution of the king in 1649 was not merely the ultimate attack upon the existing hierarchy of social order - to many it must have seemed less a merely political act than a blasphemy against God when men so raised their hands against his anointed. There were men among the regicides who held or were to hold - like Henry Lawrence - Baptist views.

The claim to a universal toleration which most sectaries, including the Baptists, tended to press seemed to many conservative churchmen, both episcopalian and presbyterian, merely a demand that every man should be free to choose his own road to hell. After the triumph at Naseby, 14 June 1645, of the New Model Army, alive as it seemed with wild swarms of sectarian opinion, many who had hitherto believed in Parliament's cause began to fear that they had unleashed a far more terrible tyranny than the king's personal rule - the rule of King Mob. University educated ministers were infuriated to find a mushroom growth of 'mechanic preachers', untaught, sometimes actually illiterate, challenging both their spiritual authority and their traditional right to the tithes which paid them. This all meant not merely a challenge to the individual person and his stipend but to the very unity of the Church in England. The Revolution made uncertain the simple age-old situation where Church and State were linked by one unquestioned partnership in which the Church supplied the cement of a common faith and the divine validation of the accustomed forms of society. This was gone completely by 1646, gone never to return. It is hardly surprising that some supporters of the traditional order failed to recognise its departure or, recognising it, refused to accept it.

Of course, there was a tendency among the sectaries' opponents to exaggerate the danger of their wilder words and deeds but there is an abundance of evidence to show the immense social unsettlement which accompanied the civil wars and the spread of radical political opinions even among very ordinary people. The exuberance of young soldiers plucked from the obscurity of rural England and pitchforked into an Army which, during the late 1640s and 1650s, became only too conscious that it alone represented authority, the naked authority of the sword, in the British Isles, was inevitable. But it meant many wild sayings and doings which deeply disturbed and sometimes terrified those who were still rooted in the old ways. Many of the sectaries in and out of the Army, consciously or unconsciously, were the agents of social revolution.

To social revolution was added a profound spiritual instability. Men's convictions grew from seedling to harvest at breakneck speed in those tumultuous years. This multiplies problems for the historian: a man might be a loyal adherent of his parish church in 1644 and then by turns a Presbyterian, Independent, a Baptist, a seeker and, before the restoration of Charles II in 1660, a Quaker. It is certainly unwise to assume that a man remained a member of that group to which he belonged at the moment when some fragment of evidence brings him to the historian's notice.

It is against this background that the politics and propaganda of the Baptists must be understood together with the resistance and the hostility to them which were sometimes displayed. Many people felt profoundly insecure during this period and those, such as the Baptists, who challenged the most vital traditions of church and state increased their unease. Infant baptism had tied church and community neatly together. Believer's baptism sundered the church, the company of the committed, both from other groups with churchly pretensions and from men's "natural" social context - the parish.

General Baptist Evangelists

Thomas Lambe was an early example of the disturbing influence of Baptist evangelists. He was a soap-boiler who seems first to have adopted Baptist convictions c.1640 in Colchester. For propagating his views he was arrested and imprisoned in London. After his release he was apparently active as an evangelist in Gloucestershire and was immersing his converts in the Severn towards the end of 1641.

By 1645 he was leading the church at Bell Alley, Coleman Street, London. Glimpses of the life of this community are provided by the hostile and not always detailed references in Thomas Edwards' *Gangraena* (1646). It seems that the church was immensely popular with younger people in the capital for, Edwards sourly admitted, 'youths and wenches flock thither'. At their public meetings, which seem to have been both lively and chaotic, the noise was 'as if it were at a play'. In consequence, on Sunday evening, members of various sectarian and other more staid congregations would join them to share the excitement of the preaching and the doctrinal debates. There were often several speakers and the gathering would sometimes shout out their preferences among the preachers on offer. Each one was open to contradiction during and after his discourse and it seems that almost any theological subject was allowable for discussion among them: election, the perfection of the saints and the immortality of the soul were all debated. Some, at least, of Lambe's women members were no sabbatarians either for they shocked their neighbours by working on Sundays commenting, 'they knew no Sabbath ... every day was alike to them and one was as good as another'. The marriage ceremony at Bell Alley was simple and did not require any minister to conduct it: the couple concerned would, in the presence of their fellow churchmembers, 'profess to take each other to live together' and someone present would record the fact with the signatures of the witnesses.

During 1645-46 Thomas Lambe seems to have had a roving commission from his church and appeared, with his associates, in Essex, Kent, Surrey, Hampshire and Wiltshire as well as in the city of London, successfully canvassing their views and infuriating the orthodox ministers.

It seems that some time in 1645 the then Lord Mayor had Lambe, and one of his fellow preachers, a twenty-year old weaver baptized as a believer six months earlier, arrested under a recent ordinance of Parliament forbidding preaching by those not ordained ministers. Lambe argued that 'he was a preacher called and chosen by as reformed a church as any was in the world'. This defence was unacceptable and he was sent before a parliamentary committee by whom, after a brief imprisonment, he was released only to preach 'more openly and more frequently than before'. Apparently the city authorities thenceforward decided it was pointless to attempt further to enforce the ordinance.[12]

After this Lambe was to be for a period a chaplain with Cromwell's army and, like several of his associates, to be involved with the Levellers. He continued to be active among the General Baptists down to his death c. 1672.[13]

Edward Barber, a citizen and merchant taylor of Threadneedle Street, London, appears to have died before the restoration but he was certainly active among the General Baptists of the 1640s. Already by 1641 he had suffered imprisonment in Newgate gaol for his opposition to infant baptism and to the demand for payment of tithes. In that year he printed a petition *To the kings most excellent majesty* in his own name claiming to speak for many 'loyal and faithfull subjects' who had been persecuted 'by the prelates and their adherents' for obedience to what they believed to be the commands of Christ. He argued that 'no man ought to be forced in matter of religion, the Gospel being spiritual and requireth only spiritual worshipers like to itself: which cannot be made so but by the Word and Spirit of God, which breatheth where and when it listeth and not where and when men's laws and statues pleaseth which may make hypocrites but not true Christians'.[14] This plea succintly summarised the main line of argument against the persecution of men for conscience sake put forward by other Baptists and sectaries of the time.

Early in the following spring Barber also produced *A small treatise of baptisms or dipping* (1642). Oddly, at this early date, he assumed without argument that 'baptism' meant 'dipping' (immersion) rather than sprinkling or some other method. On the other hand he did set out in some detail what he believed to be the Lord's intention in instituting believer's baptism. This intention was sevenfold: (i) to make us 'conformable to himself', (ii) to assure us 'he hath washed us from all our sins', (iii) that 'we have the Holy Spirit to begin all in and perfect all for us', (iv) that we are brought into 'union with the whole body of God upon earth', (v) that 'this is Christ's livery', (vi) that 'we are enabled to it by Christ', (vii) that those immersed are 'visibly sealed to the day of redemption', have a 'right to communion' and are 'crucified, dead and buried, and risen again with Christ'.[15] In 1643 Edward Barber sought to promote a petition on behalf of 'certain Christians reproachfully called Anabaptists' inviting Parliament and the divines of the Westminster Assembly to debate with them a number of doctrinal issues and, if their opponents could prove 'their ministry, baptism or sabbath to be commanded of God ... or anything we hold to be contrary to godliness, then we will thankfully be reduced to the truth and repent and revoke our errors and suffer for our presumption'. The invitation was not taken up.[16]

It is generally believed that Barber's church was one with that led by Thomas Lambe and that this was the congregation divided over 'laying on of hands' as the result of the arguments for the practice put forward within it by Francis Cornwell (a former Anglican clergyman) about 1646.[17] Cornwell had himself been baptized by William Jeffery of Sevenoaks some two years earlier. While little is known of Cornwell after 1646, Jeffery was the earliest known General Baptist leader in Kent and founder, with others, of more than twenty other congregations in that county in addition to the Bradburn-Sevenoaks church of which he was probably first pastor. He continued to affirm the necessity of laying hands upon newly baptized believers as a condition of communion.[18]

William Jeffery was to become one of the first of the 'messengers', an order of inter-church officers which the Calvinistic Baptists were also to use but never to institutionalise. As early as 1645, in *A true discovery of the ministery of the Gospell*, Edward Barber had set out the foundations of General Baptist thinking of this order of ministry. Barber believed that the office of 'apostle or messenger has not ceased'. The qualifications for office were not only that he must be converted by the work of the Spirit and a baptized member 'of a true church in the order of the Gospel' but, being capable of 'a good measure of self-denial' he should be commissioned 'by the church of which he is a member'. He must gather disciples by preaching and by baptism and plant them in the churches. At the same time messengers are to be 'servants of the churches ... not masters ... but as servants to be disposed by them'. Furthermore they are not to be a financial drain upon the churches 'therefore they that have trades let them use them and those that have none let them get into one'. Nor are they to flee persecution but to 'lay down their lives for the publishing and defence of the Gospel if God call them to it' for they must remember that they 'do represent the very presence and person of Jesus Christ'. In this little tract, which not surprisingly reads rather more like a Bible study on ministry in the New Testament than as something tested by long experience, Barber also dealt more briefly with the responsibilities of pastors, teachers and deacons, and was obviously trying to hold to a strict obedience to the New Testament pattern.[19]

Barber's last writing was also concerned in part with the ministry but here he was deeply critical of the Presbyterians who, far from being willing to accept stipends from God's people alone, found such support 'too mean and low for the plush and silken ministers of these times'. True ministers of Christ, he claimed, were equipped by God and not by Oxbridge studies: those who truly desired the full reformation of Christ's Church 'according to the Word of God' must surely grant liberty of conscience to others for, as he said in the course of reiterating the arguments he had used in 1641, it is the true Church which is a suffering community and to persecute it is a mark of the Antichrist.[20]

Samuel Oates, who is more often remembered as the father of the notorious Titus, was closely linked with Thomas Lambe and the Bell Alley church in 1646 when some of his doings were recorded by Thomas Edwards. Edwards and his correspondents were always ready to believe the worst of the sectaries and the smears used against Oates were entirely typical of the time. It was alleged that his evangelism was highly profitable to him in cash terms for, they said, he worked most successfully among impressionable women and charged the poor two shillings and sixpence for their baptism and the better-off ten shillings. In consequence, it was said, 'he came very bare and mean into Essex but before he had done his work was well-lined and grown pursie'. It was also claimed, for good measure, that when his converts were baptized they provided a feast for the church and afterwards were 'admitted to that they call the Lord's Supper'. In addition there were the customary allegations of sexual misbehaviour and reports of one occasion when he was imprisoned for a while on suspicion of having caused the death of a woman whom he had baptized. It appears that on this occasion there were other accusations, notably that he had preached against the parliamentary assessments for taxation, claiming that the saints should not be compelled to pay and that Parliament should not make laws for the saints since that was the prerogative of Jesus Christ alone.

Just how much truth there was in all this is difficult to tell. On the one hand he was publicly cleared of responsibility for the woman's death and it seems unlikely that he could have continued his career as an evangelist into the later 1640s and 1650s if serious scandal attached to him. On the other, there is no doubt that he and others deliberately catered to popular anticlericalism. They believed that both episcopalians and presbyterians, by being willing to accept state stipends and to press for state suppression of sectarian liberty, were betraying the cause of the Gospel. Hence it is entirely likely that one of Oates's congregations at Bocking in February 1646 did jeer at the constables who came to break up their meeting telling them to get them 'to their steeple house, to hear their popish priests, their baal's priests'. On the other side it is interesting that in 1646 Presbyterian ministers were complaining that magistrates in the home counties were helpless to do much to suppress the sectaries and their evangelistic activities because they received no backing from London. It is hardly surprising that some of Oates's more enthusiastic and active opponents took the law into their own hands: they dragged him from the house where he was staying in Dunmow, Essex and threw him into the river thus, recorded Edwards with unloving satisfaction, 'thoroughly dipping him'.[21]

Even such treatment did not quench Oates' enthusiasm for his evangelistic work for, in the years 1647-48, he was reported as continuously active in and around the tiny county of Rutland. In October 1647 he was arrested as 'a disturber of the peace of the state and church' and sent before Abel Barker, the sheriff of the county. In December that year a number of local ministers sent up a petition to Parliament complaining of his preaching to congregations in Rutland, Northamptonshire, Leicestershire and Lincolnshire 'in barns, stables and such unfit and unseemly places'. They objected to him preaching in seemly places also for they complained that he was 'breaking into churches and thrusting himself into our pulpits'. More seriously, perhaps, both in London's eyes and in those of the civil authorities elsewhere, was their further accusation that Oates had 'of late also dispersed and endeavoured to promote that seditious paper called the Agreement of the People'. This was one of the most important of all the earlier Leveller manifestoes. In spite of his arrest by order of the House of Lords, his escape, his re-arrest and his appearance at the Assizes in Rutland, the case for the prosecution was, due to some misunderstanding, not properly prepared and by May 1648 the ministers were again complaining that Oates was once more at work gathering 'his mutinous assemblies', proclaiming 'his blasphemous errors' and uttering 'most seditious and treasonable speeches against monarchy itself'.22

By the spring of 1649 Oates had apparently settled for a time as the pastor of a General Baptist congregation in Lincolnshire but, in the 1650s, he was with the Army in Scotland as chaplain to Colonel Pride's regiment. While there he was involved in some unrest during the winter of 1654-55 among the more radical officers who apparently wished for a more democratic government and the abolition of tithes. After this sturdy history of ecclesiastical and political radicalism it is strange that soon after the restoration he conformed for a time and accepted an Anglican living at Hastings. However, as Crosby comfortably recorded, he finally repented his apostasy and returned to membership with Thomas Lambe's congregation for the last five or six years of his life.[23]

Henry Denne was formerly a minister of the Church of England who had been ordained by the bishop of St David's about 1630 and who was curate of Pyrton in Hertfordshire during most of the 1630s. He seems to have adopted Baptist views and to have joined the Bell Alley congregation in 1643-44. The church then sent him out, according to Thomas Edwards, as an evangelist in Bedfordshire and Cambridgeshire. The parliamentary Cambridgeshire county committee took exception to his activities and sent him up to London where he was imprisoned for a short time. After this, apparently through the interest of the Disborough family, he was settled as minister of the parish church at Eltisley, Cambridgeshire, whence he drew his stipend. He was not only accustomed to revisit Bell Alley but, in December 1645, he accompanied Thomas Lambe upon a preaching tour to Rochester and Canterbury. At Canterbury they baptized an unnamed gentlewoman of whom it was later claimed that 'by dipping she was cured of an incurable disease'. Round about this time it was reported that he had turned carter believing (as it will be remembered Edward Barber had argued) that ministers 'must work with their hands and follow some worldly calling'. This phase, if truly reported, does not appear to have lasted very long and soon after he returned to Caxton, a mile from Eltisley, where he had his home. During the following June, however, he was itinerating through Lincolnshire and in Spalding was arrested by two local magistrates who found him baptizing local people at midnight.

Even Thomas Edwards had to admit that Denne's preaching against tithes helped his popularity and it is interesting also that what Edwards reported about Denne's activities at Eltisley clearly reflected what Thomas Lambe had practised at Bell Alley. No psalms were sung but Denne preached and prayed. After that any who were dissatisfied with his exposition could bring forward their objections and he would answer them. Thereafter one or two or even more of the brethren, usually 'mere mechanics', would also preach to the company.[24]

What remains mysterious in Denne's career is why, sometime between June 1646 and May 1649, he joined the army and not, it appears as a chaplain. An opponent hinted that for a while he may have been drawn to the views of those who believed that Christians should live above and beyond such carnal outward ordinances as water baptism. Perhaps also he may have seen the Army as the only possible instrument for winning toleration and other reforms such as the ending of tithes which nearly all of those in authority resisted.[25]

At all events he next appeared as one of the four Leveller leaders to be shot at Burford after the failure of the Army mutiny in May 1649. Denne alone was pardoned and, a little later, produced his explanation of his conduct in *The Levellers designe discovered* (1649). There he gave no indication that he had himself sympathised with any part of the Levellers' political aims (his title provided the only reference to them) and explained his part in the mutiny as the result of rumours which undermined his trust in the senior officers. He now recognized that he had been guilty both of failing 'to yield obedience unto that authority under which we are placed' and of not telling the Council of War his grievances before taking the extreme step of mutiny. Towards the end of the pamphlet he recognized the importance of not dividing the Army and suggested that however good the intentions of some men had been in the affair the intentions of the majority were far different. But upon the nature of those dark intentions he cast no light.

The Laying On of Hands Controversy

There is a gap in Denne's career from Burford to the opening of the Fenstanton Records which provide the most detailed account now extant of a General Baptist church in the 1650s.[26] Not only do they throw light upon Henry Denne's own activities and the congregation's internal life but they also give valuable information about the wider fellowship of the churches linked with them. It appears that Henry Denne was responsible for baptizing the first members of the church at Fenstanton in 1644-45 although detailed records do not now exist before November 1651. The church at Warboys seems also to have grown out of Denne's preaching and to have become separate from Fenstanton by 1647.[27]

In 1651 the signatories of *The faith and practice of thirty congregations* included Edmund Mayle and Thomas Coxe from Fenstanton as well as a number from the districts of Rutland, Leicestershire, Lincolnshire and neighbouring counties where Samuel Oates and, to a lesser extent, Henry Denne had been active. The 1651 Confession therefore seems particularly to reflect the influence of the two evangelists originally from the Bell Alley congregation. It is noticeable that the Confession stressed, among those doctrines involved with the church and its ministry, that believer's baptism by immersion was a condition of church membership; that church discipline should be imposed to hold members to a holy life; that poverty-stricken members should be helped 'with food and raiment'; that help could also be sought from other congregations for those in special need; that their teachers should be supported by voluntary offerings but that they ought 'to be content with necessary food and raiment and to labour with their hands that they may not be overchargeable'; that advice should be sought over unsolved controversies within individual congregations 'from some other society which they are in fellowship with'; and that the power of the magistracy, exercised 'in a just parliamentary way' should be supported 'with our estates and lives'. It is noteworthy that laying on of hands upon believers after baptism was not mentioned although this was already a matter of controversy among General Baptists and those at Fenstanton probably already practised it. This issue was to continue to be a major cause of division among General Baptists in the 1650s very much as that of believer's baptism as a condition of communion and membership was to be among Particular Baptists during the same period. It is known that, at least as late as 1655, Samuel Oates was strongly opposed to making laying on of hands a condition of communion.[28]

In September 1653, the Westby, Lincolnshire congregation wrote asking why Fenstanton refused to go and join with those who had not accepted the imposition of hands while allowing such people into membership with them. After all, they pointed out, such an apparent inconsistency, 'doth not only strengthen them in their disobedience but also exasperate and stir up the indignation of their spirits against those faithful brethren and churches that are (in this kind) unleavened'. In their reply Fenstanton justified their position by citing Rom.14.1 and Acts 18.26. Meanwhile, during the same month, Fenstanton also received a letter from the church at Thurlby, Lincolnshire, reporting that their pastor, Robert Wright, had, after coming under the laying on of hands himself, pressed them to allow him to resign as pastor. This they had done but, some months later, he also wanted to withdraw from membership with them and, once more, the laying on of hands was one of the matters about which he complained. Edmund Mayle and John Denne (Henry's son), the two Fenstanton elders, were able on this occasion to effect a reconciliation. Early in 1655 the same pair were sent, in answer to invitations from the churches at Wisbeach and Peterborough, to administer the laying on of hands to members of those congregations. At Wisbeach, however, the administration was held up because of an intervention by John Lupton and Joseph Wright from the Coningsby and Tattershall, Lincolnshire, church who argued that those who 'were under laying on of hands ought to separate themselves from those who were not under it and have no communion with them'. It is clear that passions were also rising high on the other side for a majority of the Thorpe, Rutland, congregation, including the elders, had decided 'to have no communion with those that were under laying on of hands' and had then visited Thurlby to break the unity of that congregation on the issue. Fenstanton wrote regretting these moves and reminding them that a representative gathering at Leicester had agreed that those taking either side of the controversy could and should continue to work together. A reply from Thorpe, however, indicated no inclination to compromise on the matter.[29]

But, in taking their strong and exclusive line, Lupton and Wright were not acting merely on their own initiative. John Lupton had been a member of the assembly of General Baptist leaders which had met in London during 1654 and had produced *The humble representation and vindication* affirming their loyalty to 'the powers that are in present being'. It seems, however, that other matters were also discussed and it was decided that they could on no account have communion with those who did not practise the laying on of hands. Among the messengers on this occasion were listed

Samuel Fisher, who was to defect to the Quakers the following year, William Jeffery, whose *The whole faith of man* (1659) was to argue for the assembly's position, John Lupton himself and Benjamin Morley of Ravensthorpe, Northamptonshire, whose church had belonged to Oates's sphere of influence and who had signed the 1651 Confession. First on the list of elders was the London leader John Griffiths whose *Gods oracle and Christs doctrine* (1655) was also to argue strongly for the imposition of hands upon baptized believers. This position was reaffirmed at the assembly held during September 1656 in London which represented many of the same leaders.[30]

The church at Fenstanton

Henry Denne's position in the fellowship at Fenstanton was never, apparently, clearly defined. His name stood above the numbered list of the members and he was never termed pastor. Like other senior members of the congregation he took his turn in rebuking and correcting the erring but the day-to-day leadership was manifestly in the hands of the two elders. He took two significant initiatives. In October 1653 he urged the responsibility for proclaiming the Gospel more widely upon the congregation and was, at the end of the month, himself 'chosen and ordained by the laying on of hands a messenger to divulge the Gospel of Jesus Christ'. On 3 November, accompanied by a fellow-member, he started on a ten-day preaching tour which involved some personal evangelism, preaching in a parish church in Cambridge and visiting scattered saints and house churches. Not long afterwards, perhaps as the result of the questions raised by those whom he had met, he and other leaders at Fenstanton were asked to draw up some formal doctrinal statements concerning the pressing controversies of the day. It is worth noting what these were thought to be: whether Christ died for all, believer's baptism, whether God were the author of sin, whether the ordinances of God still continued and, finally, whether believers could fall from grace.

The second initiative was taken the following November. Henry Denne was unwell so it was John Denne who told the congregation that his father had recently been in Canterbury where a group of baptized people, 'all of them out of order', that is, not organized into a church, had begged him to stay with them. Henry Denne had replied that this would depend on 'what the congregation should say to whom he belonged'. Fenstanton wrote cautiously to discover whether the brethren at Canterbury still needed his help and received an enthusiastic letter asking for Denne's release to them. The church, a little unwillingly, agreed to let him go but later expressly commissioned him and provided him with a companion, money and horses for the journey. The letter headed 'from the church of God in and about Canterbury' the following February clearly implied that the congregation was now formally established and most appreciative of him as their pastor. Denne, they reported, 'is provided of an house and we doubt not of a comfortable being and subsistence amongst us'.[31] With this he passed out of the story of the Fenstanton congregation. He published three more pamphlets, signed *The humble apology* (1661) put out jointly with the Calvinistic Baptists and died, according to Thomas Crosby, soon afterwards.[32]

But the Fenstanton records have much more to provide than sidelights on the life of Henry Denne. The early pages are largely given up to accounts of visits by the elders and others to people who eventually withdrew from membership on various grounds but, in most cases, because they claimed that their experience of the work of the Spirit was so immediate and so real that they were able to do without their former dependence upon the Bible and such ordinances as prayer, preaching, breaking bread, baptism and the laying on of hands. The messengers from Fenstanton were accustomed to warn them that 'he will not be safe, who, neglecting the scripture, resteth upon some inward inspirations above them, which oftentimes are false, but always doubtful'. People did not always entirely deny the value of ordinances: one woman explained that 'her own experience declareth that God's way is both in ordinances and out of them'. But they did desire to be free from a bondage 'to observe such outward, ceremonial and carnal ordinances'. Another woman explained, 'I cannot walk in those low dispensations for God hath manifested himself to my soul that I am his and that he is my God and that he hath done by his Spirit'. Anthony Yeule admitted that the 'Anabaptists' walked closest to the Scripture rule but, nevertheless, he did not want to continue to walk with them. Like others he was told 'That Spirit which speaks contrary to the word is not a true spirit; but that spirit which you are led by is contrary to the Scriptures; therefore, it is not a true spirit'. Such views, held by 17th century "charismatics", were the seed bed of Quakerism though they were not actually identified as those of the Quakers in the Fenstanton records until they were encountered in January 1655 at Chatteris.[33]

As has been seen, not all General Baptists shared the practice of laying hands upon the newly baptized nor were two other practices at Fenstanton universally shared - feetwashing and the holding of a church meal before the Lord's Supper. This way of arranging the Lord's Supper was discussed in January 1653 at a general meeting of the elders and brethren of the churches in the area at Cambridge. There it was ordered that, in future, all the affiliated congregations should administer the Lord's Supper at the conclusion of a fellowship meal. When, the following September, the Fenstanton church was asked by another congregation for its reasons for this practice the reply was simply that the New Testament examples were clear and that there was a practical need to provide refreshment for members who had travelled a long distance. Nevertheless, they said, they would not 'lay it upon the churches as a command from the Lord'. But, however relaxed the members with Henry Denne were over the matter, another church actually had members who withdrew from communion on the issue.[34]

Fenstanton accepted (<u>with</u> the 1651 Confession) that they should not only help with the financial support of their own poorer members but also, when necessary, the members of other churches in special need. This practice was open to abuse and Fenstanton agreed upon some rules to guide their decisions in such cases. It was decided that anyone seeking aid must explain his situation to the church or to the deacons and that the deacons should make no grant without the consent of at least two or three of the congregation including, if possible, an elder. Members should do their utmost not to allow any of their own near relatives to become a charge upon the church as a whole. Furthermore, if Fenstanton should seek the help of other churches for one of their members, they should not send the actual man in need but one 'not in want, of whose fidelity they have had experience, that he may receive their liberality and also bring it to the congregation'. Similarly, no-one from another church asking help for himself would receive a grant from Fenstanton. In fact, no-one should be helped at all until they 'to the utmost of their abilities' had used 'all lawful means for their subsistence'. As a result of these regulations two visitors were refused help in 1655 and 1657 although a member of the Dullingham, Cambridgeshire church was assisted in 1658.[35]

The way the Fenstanton congregation dealt with a disaster sustained by one of their own members, John Wilson, in the autumn of 1654 was a model of its kind. Wilson had lost his barns, outhouses, grain and hay by fire and asked whether he should go 'to the justices of the peace for the county, to desire letters of request from them to the inhabitants of the county, for the gathering of money towards the reparation of his loss'. Before a decision was taken the congregation discovered that the loss could be estimated at £30 'besides the houses which he only hired'. After some discussion the meeting decided not to recommend an appeal to the secular community but 'only to make the churches acquainted therewith'. A circular letter was forthwith drawn up asking that the churches should each send two messengers to a general meeting at the home of Arthur Hindes at Cambridge on 8 December. At this it was decided to limit the appeal to local churches and send individual contributions through Hindes. Fenstanton promised £6 and the Cambridge meeting told Hindes not to disburse the churches' gifts until Wilson had come to an agreement with his landlord about the burned buildings for they did not want to pay for those too.[36]

Margaret Spufford has written of the alienation from their natural communities experienced by dissenting villagers in Cambridgeshire in the 17th century and there can be no doubt that this would be felt all over the country. The very fact that all the General Baptist leaders required absolute separation from the Church of England as a false church must have accentuated the problem. The consequences of this worked out in various ways - one of them being the necessity for keeping their own records of marriages and births instead of relying upon the parish registers. Another was the need for a close and effective fellowship in the gathered congregation so that others would not, like one Jesper Docraw, become lonely and discouraged and so return to their parish church. Another man thought himself likely to come under economic pressure if he were baptized; he was a tenant farmer and believed he would be turned out if his landlord came to hear of it. Even the voluble, irresponsible John Blowes (who was kept from a day of prayer by a football match he had shared in organizing) <u>may</u> in part have been trying to overcome a sense of alienation from his neighbours caused by his church commitments! On the other hand the church's desire to keep itself separate from the world was another motive for taking care of its poor and for promising the secular community (as they might reasonably require) that such needy creatures as a certain Mary Whittock and her small children would not become a charge upon the parish. At the same time it was not impossible for more secular relationships to intrude into church life as when John Denne asked the congregation to rebuke his servant and fellow member, Elizabeth Noble, for disobedience and negligence. This led to her repentance but also to trouble, for a while, with her father who was also a member. The church's concern for the public reputation of its members was shown in the case of the rebuke to Thomas Green and his wife for their notorious quarrelling. The cause of the trouble was said to be Mrs Green's willingness to keep her daughter at home idle and to tolerate her petty thieving. The church urged them 'to put their daughter to service.'[37]

The Ministry among the General Baptists

During the period of the 1650s the Fenstanton records uggest that the shape of the ministry and of church office generally had not assumed a completely fixed form. Hence Henry Denne, who had been 'chosen and ordained by the laying on of hands a messenger to divulge the Gospel' in November 1653 (after, perhaps, some ten years of itinerant evangelism and church planting), was not free to take up pastoral responsibilities with the group at Canterbury without the church's permission. Nevertheless, when William Jeffery wrote in 1659 he followed Edward Barber's earlier argument that the messenger's task was to preach 'for the gathering the church and establishing of the same' and that he was the successor of the apostles. In addition it was also there made clear that the ministry was to be seen as three-fold with messengers, elders (or pastors) and deacons. Furthermore, while the church ought freely to provide maintenance for its ministers, they in their turn ought also 'to endeavour to the uttermost, to make the Gospel without charge'. The clear implication here was that ministers ought to have such occupation as would, at least partly, provide for their material needs. This seems to have been a widely held view in this early period.[38]

The two elders, John Denne and Edmund Mayle, seem to have been joint leaders of the congregation and such double leadership seems to have been common in the area. It seems to have been customary, though not invariably so, for elders to share in the ordination of officers (both elders and deacons) in other sister congregations. On occasions a meeting of elders at Cambridge would take upon itself the responsibility of sending representatives to share in ordinations and, in one notable crisis, two elders were sent to rebuke two who had become Quaker converts and 'if they did not repent, to degrade the forementioned persons from their eldership and afterwards to excommunicate them'. The two concerned did not repent and they were, consequently, degraded from their office and excommunicated. At Fenstanton there were specific rules about the right of members to preach and the rules were carefully enforced to see that individual inadequacy did not lead to any form of public scandal. Any person, it was agreed, might speak at private meetings of the church but only those who had gained the approval of the congregation might preach in public. No-one, unless actually commissioned by the church, was allowed to make it his 'sole business' to become an itinerant evangelist. It is interesting that another group of leaders was encouraged to develop in this congregation (as in Reading among the General Baptists and in South Wales among John Miles' Calvinists): four teachers who were to teach within the congregation but 'who should not meddle with the office of an elder'. It is noteworthy that, though they were recognized formally when 'prayer was made unto God for them', it was only those inducted to the Scriptural offices of deacons and elders who had both prayer and hands laid upon them.[39]

Joint Action and Organisation

The evidence for regularly organized joint consultation among the General Baptists in the 1650s is much more fragmentary than that available for the Calvinists. However, this may be due to the accident of the survival of documents in the one case rather than in the other.

There were certainly joint meetings in the East Midlands during the 1650s although it is impossible to say whether these were called occasionally for specific purposes or as part of a regular programme of association. Presumably, for example, more than one meeting lay behind the eventual production and signing of *The faith and practice of thirty congregations* (1651). It may have been, too, that the meeting at Stamford, 2-3 July 1656, at which two messengers had been commissioned as evangelists to the west country, and an earlier meeting at Leicester at which co-operation between those for and against the laying on of hands had been agreed, had been successive gatherings of an association. On the other hand, either or both meetings could have been summoned for the one particular purpose.[40]

In the Cambridgeshire area, nevertheless, it seems clear that there were both occasional and regular meetings at Arthur Hindes' home in Cambridge for joint planning and consultation 1653-55. The first, 1 February 1653, was described as 'a general meeting' at which 'the elders and brethren assembled' by whom it was 'ordered' that the Lord's Supper should be administered after a church evening meal 'throughout the congregations'. The second gathering was apparently summoned especially to consider the needs of John Wilson on 8 December 1654 and it seems to have been made up of elders only who each committed their church to a contribution - an action which was judged by the maverick pastor, Anthony Grey, of the Thaxfield congregation, 'disorderly'. Grey's refusal to contribute led to a formal complaint against him by the Melbourne church. This was taken up at the following meeting of 'the elders of several congregations' on 6 February 1655, and he was asked to attend the next meeting to answer the complaint. Meanwhile, it was agreed 'for the better attaining to, and retaining of, unity and order in the churches, that we should unite ourselves together into a strong combination, to meet often together (howsoever the elders of the respective congregations) at such times and place as should be thought most convenient'. A fourth meeting was held, 3 May 1655, at which Grey's defence was heard and rejected and he was urged to repent. It was also agreed at this meeting to send the elders John Ray and John Tabram to rebuke the elders at Littleport earlier mentioned who had turned Quakers. In Ray's letter reporting that the mission had been completed he referred to this meeting as a 'general assembly of the elders and brethren of the church of Christ at Cambridge'. At a fifth meeting, of 'the elders of several congregations', on 22 June 1655, it was agreed that it was unlawful 'for any member of the congregation to be married unto one without the congregation'. At the last meeting of elders of which a record survives, 28 September 1655, Mayle and John Denne were deputed to ordain the newly elected deacons and elders at Warboys and it was agreed that no churchmember should travel from place to place without a certificate of the advice and consent of the congregation to which he belonged, that every particular member should 'sit down with some congregation to give an account of his actions' and that every congregation should keep a register of its members.[41]

It seems clear that the elders tended to dominate meetings at Cambridge and that they may have exercised rather more power independently of their congregations than the pastors of Calvinistic churches were allowed to do at this period.

The earliest general meetings now known to have occurred in Kent were mentioned in passing by John Griffith as held at Cranbrook on 21 July 1652 and at Yalding five days later when a major debate took place on whether it was possible for a believer to fall from grace.[42]

However, the only detailed records which remain from that county concern two gatherings and the matters there 'debated and agreed upon by the messengers, elders and brethren' at Chatham, 10 March 1657 and at Biddenden, 26-27 May 1657. At the first meeting it was firmly agreed that church officers should not enlist in the army; that the evangelistic work of the messengers should be encouraged and their families provided for in their absence; that 'young gifts' of preaching should be encouraged; that the first day of the week should be set apart for worship 'seeing the servants of the Lord in the primitive churches whose steps we are to follow did meet on the first day'; and that they could not hold communion with any who denied the six principles of Hebrews 6.1f. At the second meeting emphasis was laid upon the responsibilities of elders and it was agreed 'that elders cannot fulfil their ministry on the first days of the week but also must spend some other time in visiting of the sick and seeking after the straying disciples, etc. In order to which it is further agreed that the churches are bound in duty to assist them upon that account so that they and theirs may live comfortably and furthermore that some, as helps of government, may very much help the elders in their work so that they may not leave their callings but, contrariwise, work with their hands at all seasonable times'.[43]

There were also, of course, at least three London assemblies representing the growing wing of the General Baptists who believed that it was essential to lay hands on the newly baptized. They met in 1654 and produced *The humble representation and vindication* explaining their attitudes to the civil government. In 1656 a number of matters of church discipline were dealt with while the meeting in 1660 produced *A brief confession or declaration of faith* which was to be the most widely used General Baptist statement of faith during the next generation.[44]

Attitudes to the Civil Power

The political attitudes of people, both groups and individuals, between 1640-60 were bound to change with the quite violent fluctuations of national politics. On the whole, however, most sectarians tended to desire more control of parliament by the people and something approaching complete freedom of conscience in religious matters. With that complete freedom of conscience usually went a desire for freedom from tithes and any other compulsory support of a church establishment whether episcopalian, presbyterian or independent. In the end, nevertheless, as a self-conscious General Baptist denomination began to emerge in the 1650s and its numbers grew, its corporate politics were bound to move in favour of the government in power whatever that government should be. This was largely for two reasons. First, with growth in numbers the proportion of the politically inert grew too. Secondly, the impact of the Pauline injunctions in *Romans* 13.1-7 became an overwhelming influence among a people committed to a thoroughgoing obedience to New Testament teaching which they took as legislation for all time.

Since in the 1640s there was no recognisable denomination it is only possible in those years to catch glimpses of individual leaders' political views without any certainty as to how far these were typical. At least five among the leaders seem to have shared for a while, to a greater or less degree, the ideals of the Levellers. Two or three of them actually served with the Parliamentary Army and all of them were in a situation deeply influenced by its politics and also by knowledge of the views of many other sectarians in it. The Army's mental atmosphere on occasions seems to have resembled, as Professor G E Aylmer has suggested, 'something like a mixture of a revivalist religious congress and an extreme left-wing political debating society'. The effect must have been prodigious upon those men's minds which were open to the new possibilities provided by the revolution then in progress. The Levellers, who owed much to the political ferment engendered by and reflected within the Army itself, were united in a desire for a greater measure of political democracy and religious freedom.[45]

The first of the five leaders was Jeremiah Ives, who was an active evangelist (from at least 1646 when he was with Thomas Lambe in Devizes), pastor of a congregation in Old Jewry, London, and a pamphleteer for the General Baptists over some thirty years. Whilst he seems to have been a chaplain for a period with the Parliamentary Army, he was also imprisoned in Newgate during the Autumn of 1647 for his association with a Leveller petition to Parliament.[46]

Meanwhile, Thomas Lambe the soap-boiler was active in organising support for the Levellers' 'large' petition in the Spring of 1647 and seems to have remained loyal to the cause to the end in 1649. Samuel Oates had already been seen promoting the *Agreement of the People* in Rutland during 1647 and, as was also mentioned earlier, Henry Denne was nearly executed with the Leveller leaders of the army mutiny at Burford. The fifth early leader to be involved was Edward Barber who showed his sympathies with the Leveller programme in a tract published in 1649.[47]

After the collapse of the Levellers the next serious challenge to the traditional class structure of authority came in the 1650s from the Fifth Monarchists. Although theirs was primarily a religious movement based upon the interpretation of Biblical apocalyptic, its political and social hopes reflected some of those of the Levellers. It proved distinctly attractive to a number of the Calvinistic Baptists but does not seem to have had the same influence among the Generals. Perhaps, with the beginnings of an established leadership and organisation, together with the publication of certain Confessions and other representative documents, they wished finally to be rid of the revolutionary image so widely conjured up by the term 'anabaptist'.

In the *Humble representation and vindication* (1654) its signatories made their response to the establishment of Cromwell's protectorate. They affirmed their willingness to obey 'the powers that are in present being' except in matters of religion when in obedience to God they recognised they must be prepared 'either patiently to suffer or humbly to entreat favour'. They also insisted that it was their belief that the saints would <u>not</u> rule the world until the Return of Christ. The same positions were reiterated in the Confessions of 1654 and 1660 and at the Assembly in London during 1656. In 1660 the Confession, which was presented to Charles II on 26 July, specifically opposed the support of Christian ministers by means of tithes or any other exactions by the magistrates and at the same time asserted their belief that religious persecution was 'expressly contrary to the mind of Christ'.[48]

At least three other statements involving various groups of General Baptists were put out in 1660. *The humble apology* was notable for being signed by leaders of both the General and the Particular Baptists and stressed their consistent loyalty to the government in power. *The second humble address*, signed by a group in Lincolnshire, proclaimed their defiance of a recent royal proclamation forbidding Anabaptists, Quakers and Fifth Monarchy men to assemble for worship. *The humble representation* claimed that 'although some of us were in arms under the former powers, our end was not the destruction of men's lives, but rather their preservation and to prevent the rude multitude of their designs which were no other than ruin and desolation where they did prevail'. They, too, warned that they must defy the king's prohibition of meetings for worship to discharge their obedience to God. But it was rather ironic that a group of General Baptists, some of whose early leaders had been so closely associated with the democratic ideals of the Levellers, should now be reduced to pleading their earlier intention 'to prevent the rude multitude of their designs'. Perhaps it had really been so and, if that were the case, the General Baptists were clearly no more of one mind politically than they were concerning a number of other matters.[49]

2.
The Calvanistic Baptists to 1660

The Calvinistic Baptists first appeared as a self-conscious group with the publication of their Confession in London in 1644. This was to provide the basic theological platform for their programme of evangelism, church-planting and organisation of associations for the years down to the Restoration.

The motives behind the publication of the Confession were quite explicitly apologetic for, in its preface, the writers explained that they had found themselves unjustly charged 'with holding freewill, falling away from grace, denying original sin, disclaiming of magistracy' and with 'doing acts unseemly in the dispensing of the ordinance of baptism'. Clearly their intentions were to manifest their substantial agreement with the prevailing forms of Calvinistic orthodoxy and to expound the basic elements of their doctrine of the Church. The Confession, they said, was signed by the appointed representatives of seven congregations to refute any suspicion that 'what is here published may be but the judgement of one particular congregation more refined than the rest.'

The names appended show that several of the leaders had had some experience among the underground Independent congregations which had grown up in and around London during the years before the outbreak of the Civil War in 1642. Five at least of the fifteen signatories, namely William Kiffin, John Spilsbury, Thomas Shepherd, Thomas Munden and Thomas Killcop, are known to have been, to a greater or lesser degree, involved with the family of congregations which had grown up around that founded by Henry Jacob in 1616. In addition, Paul Hobson is known to have had links with another London congregation and Thomas Patient had had experience of congregationalism in New England.

A transcript of some early papers concerned with the first beginnings of the Calvinistic Baptists makes it possible to establish something of the earlier developments which led, in the Confession of 1644, to the assertion that true Christian baptism should be administered by immersion to believers only. It appears that as early as 1630 certain rigorist tendencies appeared among the members of the Independent congregation Henry Jacob had founded in London. At its foundation this church had refused to repudiate the Church of England totally as a false church but, about 1630, it was urged by some members that it had, nevertheless, been wrong for one of their number to have their child baptised in a parish church. The majority did not agree but, eventually, on 12 September 1633 some more members, who took the stricter view and thought it wrong to have anything to do with the Church of England, were allowed to leave and form their own, stricter congregation. They were later joined by others, also apparently from Jacob's church which since 1624 had been led by John Lathrop, including Samuel Eaton who, with some others, received 'a further baptism'. The records do not explain whether Eaton and his friends were merely rebaptised at this point because they rejected their Anglican baptism or because they also believed that infant baptism was wrong anyway. However, by 1638, it is quite plain that Eaton then believed that baptism should only be administered to those able to profess their own faith. In that year a further group holding this view were released from the mother congregation, now led by Henry Jessey, to join one whose pastor was John Spilsbury.

It was not, apparently, until 1640 that Richard Blunt, who had earlier joined Samuel Eaton, raised the issue of the true mode of baptism. Blunt was not convinced that baptism should not only be administered to believers but also that it must be by immersion, 'by dipping the body into water, resembling burial and rising again' as implied by *Rom*. 6. 4. and *Col*. 2. 12. He both won the support of a number of those who had been previously baptised as believers and some members of Henry Jessey's congregation who now accepted believer's baptism. However, Jessey himself merely moved to the position that he must immerse infants. Since Blunt knew some Dutch he was sent to discuss the matter with a group in the Netherlands who, it was believed, were accustomed to immerse believers. On his return those who desired immersion as believers divided into two groups, one to be led by Blunt himself and the other by a certain Samuel Blacklock. For what happened next the evidence is somewhat ambiguous but it seems likely that Blunt first baptised himself and then baptised Blacklock. They then baptised their two sets of followers. This all seems to have taken place in the January of 1642 when some fifty-three people were baptised.[1]

Such a proceeding was bound to appear, at the very least, disorderly to other Christians and, of course, to many utterly subversive of all true order. To answer their critics the Baptists took two lines. Thomas Killcop, in answering one of the Independents, used an argument whose force he evidently believed his opponent must recognise when he urged that 'every scripture that gives you warrant... to erect a church-state, gives us the same warrant to erect baptism since the one cannot be done without the other,for none can put on Christ (that is visibly by outward profession) but such as are baptised into Christ'. The argument was simple: if Scripture gave authority for the vital act of the reconstruction of the church it must surely do so for the smaller act of reconstituting the church ordinance of baptism. John Spilsbury tackled the question from a slightly different point of view, that of the authority entrusted to a gathered congregation of believers. He claimed that when God had himself called together such a congregation, uniting them to Christ and to each other, they had the authority of Christ to choose a member or members 'as occasion offers and authorise him or them to administer baptism upon the whole body and so upon themselves in the first place as part of the same'. He then proceeded to argue that 'wheresoever a church doth rise in her true constitution, there are her ordinances and also power to administer the same; and where a thing is wanting there must be of necessity a beginning to reduce that thing again into being'. Spilsbury and his friends were not ecclesiastical anarchists, nor were his fellow signatories, nor were those who came to share the leadership in the coming years. They believed that once the apostolic pattern had been restored and the Church was once more rightly constituted neither an individual nor a congregation were at liberty to launch out upon innovations of their own.[2]

In 1642 the act of restoration was very new and the congregations so constituted lacked the cement which only time could give: in the next year or so there were to be other changes and other uncertainties in the pioneer group and it was not until 1644 that they were ready to make their first public and corporate bid for public sympathy and understanding.

The 1644 Confession

The 1644 Confession (revised in 1646) was far from being a creation *ex nihilo* since twenty-six of its fifty-three articles repeated the teaching, often with only the smallest verbal modifications, of the corresponding sections in the Separatist Confession of 1596. The basic churchmanship of the two documents was very similar: the congregation, guided by the risen Lord, possessed ultimate power to receive or to reject members and to appoint or to dismiss its officers but there were, nevertheless, significant differences.

The most obvious new feature in 1644 was the teaching given about baptism. First, it was insisted that baptism should only be administered to 'persons professing faith'.

Secondly, immersion and its meaning were stressed: it was to be 'dipping or plunging the whole body under water' as a sign of 'the washing of the whole soul in the blood of Christ', of 'that interest the saints have in the death, burial and resurrection' and as 'a confirmation of our faith, that as certainly as the body is buried under water and riseth again, so certainly shall the bodies of the saints be raised by the power of Christ, in the day of resurrection, to reign with Christ'. It was also affirmed that the administrator of baptism should be a 'preaching disciple' and, clearly reflecting contemporary controversy about the authority for the restoration of the 'lost' practice of believer's baptism by immersion, it was made clear that the right to administer was not to be tied exclusively even to the pastor much less should its practice wait upon the supply from on high of one 'extraordinarily sent'.

The second new feature in 1644 arises partly from the last point. There can be little doubt that in this Confession the position accorded to the ministry was measurably less significant than it had been among the Separatists. While both groups held that final authority lay with the whole committed congregation under the guidance of Christ the Baptists in 1644 laid less stress upon the distinctive functions of the ministry considered apart from the congregation. In 1596 there was frequent stress on the importance of the ministry, in 1644 there was hardly any. In 1596 no sacraments were to be administered until ministers had been appointed, in 1644 any 'preaching disciple' could baptise and the administration of the Lord's Supper was not even mentioned. In 1644 the ministry was considered necessary only for the 'better' well-being of the church (though in 1646 'better' was dropped)and thinking about the offices of the ministry seems only just to have begun since in 1646 the 'Pastors, Teachers, Elders and Deacons' taken over by 1644 from 1596 became, and were to remain, 'Elders and Deacons'. In fact it seems clear that in the thought of the men who drafted the 1644 Confession as with the baptism so, too, the ministry was firmly subordinated to the immediate authority of the covenanted community.

The third new feature in 1644 concerned Church-State relations. Both Confessions agreed that obedience to God was an overriding duty even if God 'with-hold the magistrate's allowance and furtherance therein'. However, while the Separatists held that it was the magistrate's duty 'to suppress and root out by their authority all false ministries, voluntary religions and counterfeit worship of God', on the one hand and, on the other, 'to establish and maintain by their laws every part of God's Word...yea to enforce all their subjects whether ecclestiastical or civil to do their duties to God and man' the signatories in 1644 seem deliberately to have avoided affirming any such link between church and state. Indeed, the statements of 1644, in view of those made in the 1596 model about the magistrate, were as important for what they did not say as for what they did. Since one motive for publication in 1644 was to refute the allegation that they were disloyal as citizens it was important for the Calvinistic Baptists to make their statements about church and state as positive as possible. So they affirmed that the secular authorities should be obeyed 'in all lawful things commanded by them' and that the Baptists were bound to defend the constitutional government which, in 1644, was 'the king and parliament freely chosen by the kingdom'. Finally, while they did not expect the state to take sides with them they asked for protection against persecution in the forms of 'wrong, injury, oppression and molestation, which long we formerly groaned under'.

These three differences, the restriction of baptism to believers, the subordination of the ministry more fully to the congregation and the severance of any links between church and state, imply a narrowing of the circle of the church even compared with that of the Separatists. It is, however, equally clear, from the expansionist policy which the Calvinistic Baptists were to pursue down to the time of the Restoration that their retreat from any traditional concept of the Christian state seems to have sharpened their sense of mission rather than to have blunted it.

A fourth new feature in 1644 was the section of twelve articles (XXI - XXXII) dealing with the life of the believer as one of God's elect. It is evident from these (for which no other literary source has yet been discovered) that, for the men of 1644, the other most significant theological event since 1596 alongside the restoration of believer's baptism had been the Synod of Dort where the new definition of Calvinistic orthodoxy had been promulgated. The twelve articles of 1644 contained or implied the five points of limited atonement, unconditional election, total depravity, irresistible grace and the perseverance of the saints although unconditional election had been asserted somwhat earlier. This whole section, whatever its origin, was introduced into the framework provided by the 1596 Confession by men who took the Calvinistic orthodoxy of their day with great seriousness. The very scissors-and-paste method used by the compilers of the 1644 Confession makes it clear that every part of it had been most carefully scrutinised before inclusion. Hence it must be recognised as the fundamental expression not merely of the doctrines connected with the central theme of the nature and organisation of the visible church, but also of the faith which these men desired to see propagated throughout the British Isles and New England during the years to come.[3]

The Origin and Theology of Associations

A last and very significant feature of the 1644 Confession derived directly from that of 1596 and dealt with inter-congregational relationships. Article XLVII in 1644 was a verbatim transcript of Article 38 in 1596. It read as follows: 'And although the particular congregations be distinct and several bodies, every one a compact and knit city in itself, yet are they all to walk by one and same rule and by all means convenient to have the counsel and help of another in all needful affairs of the church, as members of one body in the common faith under Christ their only head'. In 1644 this article was equipped with more scriptural proof texts than in 1596 which all tended to stress apostolic examples of common faith and practice and included one reference to the financial support given by one congregation to another. In the 1646 edition the texts were again revised and now included a reference to the council at Jerusalem, *Acts* 15, and more references to financial assistance between churches.

Both the use of the 1596 article and the supply of new proof texts bore witness to the active concern of the men of 1644 with unity of doctrine, polity and action among their churches and their recognition that the tool for building that unity was 'the counsel and help one of another'. Unity would be found, of course, in the study of the Bible as laying down the 'one rule'. Here, in embryo, were the convictions which underlay the development of the 'association' of individual churches in a district or region which was to be a key structure in the expansionist policy of the years 1644-1660.

By 1644 there were several ways in which the first London Particular Baptists were being encouraged to closer co-operation. First, several of their leaders had experienced vital inter-congregational links among the Independent churches to which they had formerly belonged. Secondly, they were evidently taking very seriously the biblical ideals enshrined in Article XLVII of their Confession. Thirdly, their tendency to cling together and to work together would be all the greater because the label 'Anabaptist' made them virtually outcasts from the wider fellowship of English puritanism. Fourthly, earlier in 1644, John Cotton's book, *The keyes of the kingdom of heaven* had appeared in London with a preface by the Independents, Thomas Goodwin and Philip Nye. In both the preface and the body of that book ideas of 'association' and 'consociation' between individual congregations were encouraged and taught. Strangely, associations became the characteristic units of Baptist organisation from the 1650s but did not among the English Independents until the 19th Century.

A suggestion about the origins of associations first made by W T Whitley has more recently been given wide currency and fresh exposition by R G Torbet in the following terms:[4]

> The pattern of the more formal associational organisation, as it was worked out, was provided by a military expedient with which Baptists had become familiar during the Civil Wars (1642 -49) between King and Parliament. During that first winter, counties were organised into "associations" for defence purposes. This plan was adapted to raising money and troops from the counties. Then Cromwell's New Model Army, thus organised, brought into being a council for political action and protection of communities against plunder, to which each regiment sent representatives. In 1653 that part of the army that was disbanded in Ireland, and which was largely composed to Baptists, transferred this plan to church organisation as they sought to maintain fellowship between their lonely congregations in a strange country by correspondence and the frequent meeting of delegates. These Irish associations sought contact with Welsh, Scotch and English Baptists who were attempting a similar type of inter-church communication.

It will not be necessary to make any comments on the accuracy of this description of the organisation of the Parliamentary army under Cromwell but it is necessary to deal in detail with this as a suggestion about the origin of associations. In this form the theory appears to be based upon the common use, by Parliament and the Calvinistic Baptists, of the term 'association' with its link to a specifically 'county' organisation. But the actual word 'association' does not seem to have been much used among the Baptists even during the 1650s: they preferred to use the term 'General Meeting' for the periodic gatherings of their representatives or, as they normally termed them, 'messengers'. Secondly, the Baptist associations of the 1650s were regional far more than county in their constituency. Thirdly, the scheme launched by Parliament in the winter of 1642-43 had very little in common with the inter-congregational co-operation of the Baptists apart from the rather remote parallel afforded by Parliament linking their supporters among the country gentry together at all. The second step in this theory of the origin of associations is taken by citing the appearance of regimental representation on Cromwell's army council in 1647. This seems especially superfluous when it is remembered that, three years earlier, the 1644 Confession had itself been signed by 'some of each body in the name, and by the appointment of seven congregations'. The final step in the argument was connected with the letter from the Irish Baptists (whose numbers were probably not as great as Dr Torbet seems to suppose) with accompanying documents in June 1653. There, it should be noted, the word 'association' does not appear, there is no mention of a series of meetings or even of one general meeting, the suggestion was that a correspondence should be developed and that, although members of three Irish churches were signatories, the letter was sent as from the church at Waterford. As will be seen later in this chapter, general meetings of churches were already being held in at least three areas outside London and the real contribution of the

Irish letter was the suggestion of a monthly national fast day for all the Calvinistic Baptists. This idea was taken up in the churches all over Britain.[5]

Incidentally, they did not at this period refer to themselves as Calvinistic Baptists but as 'the churches of Christ walking in the faith and order of the Gospel' or as 'the baptised churches'. While the term 'Anabaptist' applied to them by others was intended not only to link them with the half-remembered stories of atrocities by Anabaptists at Munster a century earlier but also to insist that they were re-baptisers, their own term for themselves, 'the baptised churches', clearly implied that other Christians were not, in their eyes, baptised at all!

The appearance of the London Confession with its signatories explicitly representing specific churches provides the earliest evidence of a gathering of 'elders and messengers' such as would become, during the 1650s, the common pattern of association meetings. While the London leaders worked together from at least 1644 onwards the first 'General Meeting' now known in the provinces did not take place until November 1650. Nor is it known who first realised that it was not enough to send out evangelists from London to win converts and plant churches but that tiny, isolated congregations would be immeasurably strengthened if their leaders could regularly 'have the counsel and help one of another in all needful affairs of the church'. What is clear from the surviving records is that from the first the support of weaker congregations formed an important part of the delegates' concerns and that the 'General Meeting' became the regular court of appeal for struggling churches seeking advice or other help.

The development of the thinking of the Calvinistic Baptists about the theology and purpose of association before the Irish letter can be illustrated from an agreement, confirmed and subscribed by the representatives of five churches gathered at Tetsworth, Oxfordshire, in March 1653, who were in close touch with the London leadership. The moving spirit appears to have been Benjamin Cox, a former clergyman, one of the signatories of the 1646 revision of the 1644 Confession. This agreement first stated that 'true churches of Christ ought to acknowledge one another to be such and hold a firm communion each with other'. This 'firm communion' was to be worked out in three areas of their life: (i) in providing advice over controversial matters which an individual church found itself unable to settle alone, (ii) in the financial assistance of any congregation in need and, (iii) in planning, 'as need shall require and as shall be most for the glory of God to the joint carrying on of the work of the Lord that is common to the churches'.

At the same time two major theological principles were stated as the basis of such inter-congregational co-operation. First, the necessity for association between individual congregations was affirmed to be the same as that compelling association between individual believers in a single gathered congregation: 'there is a like relation betwixt the particular churches each towards other, as there is betwixt particular members of one church. For the churches of Christ do all make up but one body or Church in general under Christ their head...And in his body there is to be no schism which is then found in the body when all the members have not the same care one over another. Wherefore, we conclude that every church ought to manifest its care over other churches as fellow members of the same body of Christ in general'. The second principle was stated along lines which ran somewhat parallel to the first: if, as was generally agreed to be the case, a major motive for membership of an individual congregation was 'to keep each other pure and to clear the profession of the Gospel from scandal', the same motive must also operate to encourage individual congregations to have fellowship together. Hence, unless 'orderly churches be owned orderly and disorderly churches be orderly disowned', the visible church could not be kept pure, nor could the profession of the Gospel be kept from scandal.[6]

The one unifying document for the whole outreach policy of the Calvinistic Baptists during this period was the 1644 Confession with its modifications in 1646 and 1651 and the reprints in London in 1652 and in Scotland in 1653. At the same time there were inter-association links by letters, reports of discussions and by delegates from one association to another. The whole structure was held together by the London leaders.

The first leaders of the Calvinistic Baptists

The signatories of the 1644 Confession published while the outcome of the Civil War was still uncertain, included several men whose leadership in the years which followed was to be growingly important. The first was William Kiffin (1616 -1701). Kiffin was the only Calvinistic Baptist whose considerable wealth and principled commitment to obedience to 'the powers that be' was to keep him in close touch with the government from Cromwell to James II. He had been orphaned during the great plague of 1625 and had been a near penniless apprentice during the years thereafter who gradually got caught up in London's pre-civil war sectarian Christian underworld. He was a year or two younger than his friend John Lilburne but never seems to have shared his taste for radical politics. After coming to Baptist convictions about 1642 he came to be pastor of the congregation he was to lead from at least as early as 1644 for the rest of his life. He signed most of the important published and unpublished documents of the Calvinistic Baptists for half a century and continued to be one of their trusted counsellors into old age. He was to become particularly well known among them for his steadfast rejection of 'open membership', for his opposition to Fifth Monarchy politics and to state payment of Baptist ministers. His wealth was considerable, even during the 1650s; he became Member of Parliament for Middlesex 1656-58, master of the Leathersellers Company of London 1671-72 and an alderman of the City in 1687.[7]

Thomas Patient signed the Confession with Kiffin as a leader of the same church. While in New England he had come to reject infant baptism and had consequently found it best to leave Massachusetts sometime in the late summer of 1642. Probably after 1644 but before he also signed the 1646 edition of the Confession he was involved with Kiffin in an unsuccessful mission to Kent where their converts were taken over by the General Baptists. He seems to have stayed in London until early in 1650 when he joined the English invasion of Ireland. There he played a prominent part in building Baptist congregations only returning to England at the restoration. Then, after a period helping the Pithay, Bristol, closed membership Calvinistic Baptists he returned to London where he began work once more as a colleague of William Kiffin but died of the plague in 1666.[8]

John Spilsbury (d. 1668?) was the earliest of the signatories of the 1644 Confession to preach and practice believer's baptism and his pamphlet *A treatise concerning the lawful subject of baptisms* (1643) is the first known publication on the subject by a Calvinist. Spilsbury seems to have remained in London throughout the 1650s and to have shared the London leadership particularly closely with William Kiffin. It seems probable, from the pieces in which they appeared co-signatories, that he shared Kiffin's loyalty to moderate policies and to Cromwell.

Paul Hobson signed the Confession of 1644 and its revision in 1646 with Thomas Gower as, presumably, leaders of a congregation in London also. But from at least as early as the spring of 1644 Hobson was an army officer. He was active in evangelism in Exeter during 1646, and about the same year in Suffolk where he met and temporarily introduced to Baptist views the young Lawrence Clarkson, later to become a notorious Ranter. With Gower Hobson founded a Baptist church in Newcastle which clashed with the evangelist Thomas Tillam sent by the London church led by Hanserd Knollys during 1653. Hobson kept in touch with Kiffin but found himself suspected (with some justice) of plotting against the monarchy after the restoration in 1660 and spent time in and out of gaol until his release in 1665 on condition he went into exile in Carolina. He apparently died the following year.[9]

The modifications made in the revised Confession of 1646 were few and they may well have been, as has long been believed, largely put in to meet the objections of the Church of England apologist, Daniel Featley.

Hanserd Knollys (?1599-1691) had been an Anglican clergyman and, like Thomas Patient, had returned from Massachusetts. It appears, however, that by 1645 he had himself been baptised as a believer and had gathered round him a Calvinistic Baptist church. He signed the 1646 edition of the Confession and was to work with the Calvinists for the remainder of his life sharing the difficult times of persecution as well as the dawn of a new day in 1688. His sympathies were probably closer to the politics of the Fifth Monarchists than were Kiffin's but the two men were closely associated for over forty years: Knollys shared in the ordination services for three successive co-pastors with Kiffin - Patient in 1666, Daniel Dyke in 1668 and Richard Adams in 1690. Knollys' chief interests were in teaching, especially Latin and the two Biblical languages, and the exposition of Scripture.[10]

HANSERD KNOLLYS

After the 1646 publication one of the new signatories, Benjamin Cox, like Knollys a former Church-of-England clergyman, published *An appendix to a confession of faith* (1646), which was evidently intended not merely to expound his personal views but those of the whole group more fully in answer to certain questions which had been raised by some who had read the Confession. In it Cox explained that the writers believed that the lost suffered an eternity of torment, that Christ only died for the elect and that a true believer would be saved with or without baptism 'yet in obedience to the command of Christ every believer ought to desire baptism, and to yield himself to be baptised according to the rules of Christ in his word'. He also explained that the Calvinistic Baptists 'do not admit any to the use of the supper, nor communicate with any in the use of this ordinance, but disciples baptised, lest we should have fellowship with them in their doing contrary to order'. This point had not been made in 1644 but, whether or not it was held explicitly then, this was the position firmly taken from 1646 onwards throughout the period down to 1660. This did not mean, however, that there were no personal friendships between this group of Baptists and those who, like Henry Jessey[11] and John Tombes[12] included those holding both views of Baptism within their congregations. The latter, however, tended, if they organised intercongregational cooperation at all, to organise separately or with the Independents during this period.

Perhaps, nevertheless, the most important section was that where, equipped by the relevant scripture references, Cox explained that a disciple stirred up by the Spirit within to preach the Gospel 'is a man authorised and sent by Christ'. Those converted by his preaching 'from unbelief and false worship' are to be 'brought into church fellowship'. Such a man not only has the right to administer baptism and the Lord's Supper 'but may also call upon the churches, and advise them to choose fit men for officers, and may settle such officers so chosen by a church, in the places or offices to which they are chosen, by imposition of hands and prayer'. This passage is significant not merely because it set out the programme to be followed by a number of evangelists during missions sponsored by the London Churches during the 1640s and 1650s but because of what it did not say. This early exposition omitted to stress that the preachers concerned must only be sent out by a church which had tested their gifts for the work and that they could not go out on their mission merely on the basis of their own inward sense of call. Just as it had been proved necessary to underline such matters as the policy of 'closed communion' it was soon to become necessary also to bring the preachers firmly under control of church meeting. After reiterating once more their recognition that 'as yet we know but in part and do therefore wait upon God for further light' Cox closed his work with an assertion that faith in Christ did not dissolve other bonds whether of servants to masters, or within families or those of citizenship.[13]

Thomas Collier, who, by 1646, was already well launched upon the mission which was to engage most of his energies for the remainder of his life in the West Country, may have been one of the earliest evangelists who had not been properly commissioned by a church. This would certainly explain the curious occasion when, at a meeting held in Bridgwater during May 1654, there was considerable discussion concerning 'the more orderly ordaining of brother Thomas Collier for the performance of that work that he hath been a long time exercised in, namely in gathering and confirming the church'. While some of the brethren present appear to have been uncertain whether this should be done by the laying on of hands there seems to be have been a unanimous desire 'to proceed in a further and more orderly ordaining and appointing our dearly beloved brother Thomas Collier in the name of our Lord Jesus and of his churches who were one in it, to the work of the ministry in the world and to the churches'. This was done.14

In 1647, perhaps as a result in part of the slanders (and truths) contained within Thomas Edwards *Gangraena*, a group of Congregationalists and Baptists published *A Declaration* among whose signatories were Jessey, Kiffin and Knollys. They explained what they meant by their desire for liberty: 'that while men behave themselves peacably and justly, as touching civil conversation...they should not suffer in their names, bodies, or estates, from the hands of the civil magistrate, or any other men whatsoever, merely for what they conscientiously do, in things pertaining to the worship of God'. Furthermore, they explained that they supported the civil magistracy as appointed by God for the purpose of disciplining fallen man. Reaffirming the class structure of the time, they claimed 'that the ranging of men in several subordinate ranks and degrees is a thing necessary for the common good of men'. Following on from this they also claimed that it was contrary to Scripture and to the expression of a proper Christian compassion for people not to have their own private property. Any talk of community goods was far from their minds. Finally they utterly rejected any belief in polygamy. What is both interesting and significant is that these men felt it unnecessary to put out formal disclaimers of this kind. It is clear that they felt their work was being damaged by the allegations which had been published about them.[15]

In the light of all this, however, it is hardly surprising that when the Levellers were trying to win support among the sectarian congregations in London (and it will be remembered they had some considerable support among the General Baptists) a group of Calvinistic Baptists, led by William Kiffin himself, hastily disavowed the pamphlet, *The Second Part of England's new chains discovered* (1649), which had been read in a number of London congregational gatherings on 25th March. Hence, 2 April 1649, William Kiffin was sufficiently disturbed to lead a group of petitioners to the House of Commons to insist 'that our meetings are not at all to intermeddle with the ordering or altering civil government (which we humbly and submissively leave to the supreme power),but solely for the advancement of the Gospel'. The House graciously recognised the sincerity of the petitioners and gave them permission to publish their petition. There is no doubt that Kiffin and some of the other London leaders generally sought a reputation for respectability and a separation of their activities from any secular political commitments. Yet there is a sense in which in the 1650s the further from London the further the political involvement went and it is abundantly clear that not everyone agreed with the cautious Kiffin.[16]

The spring of 1649, with everyone needing to adjust to the tremendous blow struck against the traditional order with the execution of the King in January, must have been a rather alarming time even for those who were radical politicians, even more alarming for those who believed that politics and the Gospel really could be separated. However, in the high summer of the same year, the London Calvinistic Baptists did launch an evangelistic mission which, very largely, was free of political overtones - except that, as some were later to point out, the evangelists were supported with state pay. But that concern came later.

In September 1649, John Miles and Thomas Proud were dispatched from London to Glamorgan to gather 'a company or society of people holding forth and practising the doctrine, worship, order and discipline of the Gospel according to the primitive institution'.

They gathered five congregations and when the first three had been formed they held the first general meeting of members of the three churches at Ilston, Glamorgan on 6 - 7 November 1650. Records survive of five other such general meetings the last of which was held 30-31 August 1654.

At the same time if, as seems very likely, the internal arrangements made for the Ilston church were typical of those made for the other congregations, considerable care was taken so to organise meetings that the scattered members were in some degree held together. On 16 October 1650, for example, it was agreed that the whole church should meet to 'break bread together at Ilston' on every third Sunday. On the other Sundays the members should meet in three district groups and each district group was to hold a further weekday meeting. At the weekday meetings special care was to be taken 'to counsel, admonish, exhort and faithfully to reprove one another'. Any serious matters concerning the discipline of the fellowship would be referred to a full church meeting to be held in Ilston every third Wednesday when, in addition to carrying through any necessary business, two or three of the brethren should practice their preaching by exercising 'their gifts in private before the church'. On 14 May 1651 the church decided that, to prevent the preaching of unsound doctrine by inadequately instructed or inadequately gifted members, only those brethren should be permitted to preach at public meetings who were 'approved prophets by the church'.

In 1657 new regulations for the church's life at Ilston were agreed. These generally followed and reaffirmed earlier decisions but one very significant change was made which may have developed earlier but only then found a formal record. Before the now monthly communion service at Ilston the church officers, together with those 'as are approved prophets or upon trial for prophecy or called forth by the church, or in their courses appointed to exercise their gifts in the church', were to meet for discussion and, when necessary, decisions about discipline and the spending of the church's money. Apparently, recognised preachers and teachers in the church formed an additional circle of the spiritually mature with the elders and deacons.

There is some evidence that neither the idea of a church divided into geographical groups of members nor the development of a group of preachers to assist the elders and deacons in the administration of the church's affairs was peculiar to John Miles. As has already been noted considerable emphasis was laid by these early Baptists on unity of practice and organisation.[17]

The year after John Miles had been commissioned as evangelist and church planteer the London leaders published a further pamphlet. It was entitled *Heartbleedings for professors abominations* (1650) and was later reprinted with the 1651 and 1652 editions of the 1644 Confession. It was signed first by John Spilsbury, then by William Kiffin and afterwards by fourteen others. It was intended as a warning to 'all that profess the fear of the Lord to watch over their own hearts and ways'. There were those going about, the pamphlet warned, who asserted that salvation by the cross of Christ was a 'mere history and shadow' and that 'the scriptures are but a letter and the ordinances of God but fleshy forms, thereby labouring to beget in people's minds a contempt and slight esteem of Christ, his word and ordinances'. The arguments set out against such assertions, and further claims that traditional standards of holy living were no longer applicable, were very much on the defensive. The London Calvinistic Baptist leaders were not only warning their own constituency against such positions but were also anxious to assert that while some of those holding such views had been 'members of our congregations' they were not at all characteristic of those who held Baptist views. Indeed, they claimed, that 'though some eminent professors of the same truth with us have fallen foully' into these errors of faith and practice such people had always, when detected, been excommunicated. To the charge that they had thereby proved themselves uncharitable, the authors and signatories sharply affirmed that 'true love and charity is not the soothing of any in their sins'.[18]

Thus was the first shot discharged officially in the long struggle between the Calvinistic Baptists and the Ranters and their successors among the early Quakers. The Baptists were especially vulnerable to the charge of making an idol of the literal performance of Christian baptism with their stress on immersion as the mode and upon believers as its true subjects. There were, for example, those like William Ebury (d.1654) who cheerfully accepted that the Baptist position was closest to that of the New Testament but who argued that to be right about an empty form void of the living presence of the Spirit of God, as he believed their baptism to be, was to be tragically adrift from the reality of the matter.

Ireland and leadership outside London

Meanwhile, during 1649 and 1650, Cromwell and his troops had been active in reducing Ireland to an unwilling obedience to the English government. The Irish garrisons soon developed their own Baptist congregations in a number of places - largely made up by the invaders rather than by the native people. It was Ireland that was to cause the London Calvinist Baptist leaders considerable headaches since the politics of the Irish Baptists were well to the left of those like William Kiffin who remained at home in London.

Such embarrassments were still in the future when, in October 1652, the first moves were taken towards the forming of the Abingdon association, and in December 1652 Thomas Tillam was given authority as a messenger from Hanserd Knollys' church in Coleman Street, London, to evangelise in the North-East of the country. Thomas Collier also was apparently pondering the formation of another association about this time in the West Country of churches linked with him either because he had been responsible for their formation or through other ties.

On 24 July 1653 a letter went to Calvinistic Baptist congregations throughout the British Isles over the signatures of a number of the London leaders including, especially, William Kiffin. With the letter they sent copies of the documents they had recently received from the Irish Baptists urging that the recipients should 'communicate the same to all our beloved brethren near you and, with all convenient speed, to certify us not only what effect the the subject therein contained hath wrought upon your hearts but also a particular account of theirs and your estates and conditions with relation to your communion each with other...In order whereunto we intreat your care and pains in visiting the several weak and scattered brethren in your parts, that from a thorough knowledge of and acquaintance with their present standing we may receive information from you and our brethren in Ireland according to their desires, from us'.

As has been pointed out already the effect of the Irish letter was not, directly, to cause the formation of associations but to stir the London leadership to begin seriously to collect for the first time details of the churches in England, Scotland and Wales who could be and should be in communion with them. The Irish letter, dated, Waterford 1 June 1653, was addressed to 'the churches of Christ in London when assembled'. It was brought together with two other documents by John Vernon, an army officer from Ireland who had signed *Heartbleedings* with the London leaders in 1650. One dealt with matters the Irish Baptists believed needed prayer among the churches and the other gave details of nine existing Calvinistic Baptist congregations together with some concerning another which was likely to be founded at Carrick Fergus. In the letter itself the writers reported their decisions to have a monthly day of prayer kept by their churches on the first Wednesday (a plan which was adopted by the churches linked with John Miles) and to revive the links between them by a regular correspondence. They then made three requests of the London leaders. First that they would write once a quarter to Ireland describing their spiritual situation; secondly, that they would provide a list of the churches in England, Scotland and Wales with which they were in communion; thirdly, that they would send two or more men 'well acquainted with the discipline and order of the Lord's house and that may be able to speak seasonable words suiting with the needs of his people, to visit, comfort and confirm all the flock of our Lord Jesus that are...under his rule and government in England, Scotland and Wales'.[19]

Meanwhile, at the fifth general meeting of the Abingdon association held at Tetsworth, Oxfordshire on 10 June 1653, led by Benjamin Cox and John Pendarves among others, a letter was sent to 'the church of Christ of which our brethren John Spilsbury and William Kiffin are members and to the rest of the churches in and near London, agreeing with the same church in principles and constitutions' announcing that they had entered into a formal 'association each with other' upon the basis of the agreement of which they sent a copy and whose fundamental basis and areas of cooperation were described earlier.[20]

Benjamin Cox's career was surveyed by W T Whitley in an article[21] published many years before the Abingdon Association manuscript came to light and he noted the gap in the records for Cox's career in the late 1640s and the 1650s. This gap is now substantially filled: Cox was active in the affairs of the Abingdon Association until the division, on grounds of distance, of that association into two which was formally recognised at the Tetworth meeting on 30 March 1658. Thereafter he served the new association originally formed of the Kensworth, Eversholt, Pyrton and Hemel Hempstead churches and only visited Abingdon association meetings as their representative. Earlier he and John Pendarves had been appointed at the December 1654 meeting to visit the newly proposed Midland Association to which papers giving the Abingdon Association's grounds of association were also sent.[22] It seems that Cox continued to attend the Midland Association meetings even after they were well launched and, indeed at the September 1657 meeting of the association, Cox was charged with the task of writing to Richard Harrison to explain the arguments against the latter's willingness to accept state pay.[23]

While it is not clear whether John Pendarves, pastor of the Abingdon church 1650 - 1656, ever actually attended any of the meetings of the Midland Association there is no doubt that he was active in keeping up the links with Thomas Collier's association in the West Country. His earliest known links as a Baptist in the West Country were with Dartmouth in the winter of 1651 - 52. His wife was Thomasina Newcomen, daughter of a merchant there and aunt of the famous engineer and later Dartmouth Baptist pastor, Thomas Newcomen. In February 1654 the church at Kilmington sought Pendarves as their pastor and two months later he and another member of the Abingdon church were present at Bridgwater for Collier's ordination. He was almost certainly present at Bridgwater again in April 1655 and, at the next two meetings of the Western Association, he signed the letter to the churches with Thomas Collier. In September 1656 he died and his funeral in Abingdon appears to have been the occasion for a gathering of a number of his friends most of whom definitely held the Fifth Monarchy views with Pendarves had himself shared. The government appears to have feared the launching of an armed rising and over-reacted by breaking up the gathering with a troop of cavalry. There is every reason to believe that, like Henry Jessey and Hanserd Knollys, who also seems to have held mild Fifth Monarchy views, John Pendarves was more interested in the near approach of the Lord's Return as a spur to evangelism and church planting than as something to be prepared for by armed rebellion.[24]

There can, however, be no doubt that one did not have to be an extremist to be distinctly uneasy as a Baptist when the Barebone's Parliament of the Saints was dissolved in December 1653 and Oliver Cromwell was made Lord Protector. For those of firmly republican ideals the installation of a quasi-monarchy with, as the months passed by, more and more of the outward trappings of a traditional court, was deeply disturbing. In Ireland a number of the influential army officers were Baptists and that party was undoubtedly far more powerful there than at home in England. To them Kiffin, Spilsbury and Joseph Sansom wrote a calming letter dated 20 January 1654, saying that they had heard that the recent constitutional changes had aroused 'great dissatisfaction and opposition' and that the Irish Baptists proposed 'to make a public protest'. Not only did the London authors urge subjection to the new civil power but argued that it had been necessary for Cromwell to take firm steps to assume control because of 'the great disesteem that all power began to be in, by reason of the ill management of it in the hands where it was'. From this it appears that Kiffin and his fellow signatories were no great admirers of the Parliament of the Saints. The writers then launched an attack upon the Fifth Monarchists, because these were convictions to 'which many of those lately in power adhered'. There is some evidence that this letter was effective in restraining the army officers in Ireland. A recent discussion of the part played by the Baptists in Ireland during the 1650s seems rather too much coloured by Henry Cromwell's faintly paranoid correspondence with John Thurloe in London to give an entirely adequate picture of the realities of the situation.[25]

That there were limits beyond which John Spilsbury's loyalty to the Lord Protector would not go appears in a further letter signed by a number of the Baptist leaders in London with the Independent, John Goodwin, when, in the spring of 1657, there was widespread public discussion and support for the offer of the crown to Cromwell. Among the signatories to this letter, dated 2 April 1657, were Henry Jessey, Hanserd Knollys, John Spilsbury, Edward Harrison (pastor of the Petty France congregation in London until his death c.1674), and Joseph Sansom. Significantly, William Kiffin was not among them. In the letter they stressed their loyalty to Cromwell and their share in a common cause over many years both as soldiers at his side and as those who had prayed for it. Their horror was, they said, all the greater at the thought that the institution of monarchy should be restored which parliament had rightly declared, as recently as 1649, was 'unnecessary, burdensome, and destructive to the safety and liberty of the people'. Hence, they wrote, 'We beseech you, in the bowels of Jesus Christ, remember what God did for you and for us at Marston Moor, Naseby, Pembroke, Preston, Tredah, Dunbar and Worcester, and upon what grounds, also what boasts we have made of God thereupon, and give not cause for the enemy to say, that because God is not able to perfect his work, therefore we must return into Egypt'. It was a powerful appeal and powerfully argued. With many writing and speaking along similar lines and others arguing against restoration of monarchy in terms of simple political expediency, Cromwell was encouraged to refuse the crown.[26]

It is still widely believed that most Baptists, both Arminians and Calvinists of this period were committed to extreme left wing views. In fact, while the majority of the leading Calvinistic Baptists were probably republican in their political sentiments there must have been many who hardly had any political opinions at all. Revolutionary militancy was most likely to be found among those who held Fifth Monarchy views and who looked forward to the coming reign of Christ upon earth as the fulfilment of the prophecies in Daniel 2. Since they believed that England would be the centre of the stage upon which the events would take place which would wind up all human history, they eagerly identified events in their own recent history with the symbols of the Bible pointing, as they believed, to that final crisis. Hence, for example, to many enthusiasts, the execution of Charles I symbolized the end of the fourth monarchy and the near approach of Christ's return. It was, therefore, hardly surprising that Oliver's quasi-monarchy seemed to them not merely an interruption in the divine programme but a usurpation of the crown rights of the Redeemer. From such a conviction it was but a short step to another: that the power which Oliver Cromwell represented was that of the antichrist. Those who shared such apocalyptic speculations as these were not only divided over the exact dates but other details concerning the fulfilment of biblical prophecy. They were also divided, far more dangerously, over whether they should take an active, even violent, part in helping to inaugurate the events leading to the final catastrophe. In consequence, the Fifth Monarchy movement represented a wide spectrum of opinion from harmless Bible students constructing personal diagrams of the divine intentions to men whom the governments had real reason to fear as revolutionary activists.

Even among those who favoured Fifth Monarchy views there were therefore wide differences of approach and it is quite possible that the views of individuals may from time to time have fluctuated considerably. There is some evidence to believe that both John Vernon and William Allen, who were powerful army officers in Ireland (Allen had become a Baptist by, at latest, January 1652) may have shared Fifth Monarchy views and they were certainly strong republicans. Allen was personally fond of Cromwell but toward the end of 1654 he returned to England for an interview with him at which he seems to have made plain his hostility to the institution of the protectorate. Although in the autumn of 1655 he returned to Ireland, in December 1656 he and Vernon resigned their commissions and returned to England. In May 1658 both men attended the Western Association meeting at

Dorchester and the government spies whose report is the only record we have for the meeting told Thurloe that the evening after their arrival for the gathering 'a great contest arose about their joining with the Fifth Monarchy men but for that time not concluded by reasons of Captain Kiffin's opposing it'. Kiffin was a captain in the London trained bands, and known as a supporter of the Protector but the spies' thought appears to have been that Allen and Vernon were arguing for the Fifth Monarchy men. Whether they were right or not is another matter, for even their information that this was the issue debated was clearly secondhand.[27] Just before the Restoration, in September 1659, however, Vernon and Allen joined with a number of others in publishing *An essay toward settlement upon a sure foundation*, which denounced government by a single person, demanded the repentance of those who had supported it in the past and sought a number of legal and electoral reforms. In April 1661 both men were exiled and Allen's own last traced appearance in the records of the time was when he joined with others to contribute an elegy on Vernon who died 29 May 1667.

Once again it seems that Baptist radicals stopped short, well short, of any violent attempt to overthrow the Protectorate even when they held Fifth Monarchy views. The Midland Association meeting held in October 1656 at the church at Tewkesbury, Gloucestershire, had asked 'What is the duty of believers at this day towards the present powers, whether in civil things to submit unto them and to live what in them lieth peaceable under them?' The messengers responded with the advice that the churches should certainly live peaceably and be obedient, 'in civil things'. However, should the authorities give unlawful commands (presumably on religious matters) the messengers insisted that, 'we ought rather to suffer patiently for our just refusing to yield any active obedience to them than to rise up in rebellion against the magistrate'. They followed this advice with what they evidently believed to be a question expecting an affirmative answer: 'When the Lord shall make his people a smiting people, will he not first clearly put a just and lawful power and authority into their hands or cause such a power to be at their sides and to command them?'[28] It is perhaps even more significant that the Abingdon Association, with which John Pendarves was himself so intimately involved, did not apparently raise or discuss such questions at any point either before or after his death. It seems in fact very clear that a number even among the Calvinistic Baptists were in the end not deeply concerned with revolutionary politics at all. It is likely that most belonged to that silent majority who by abstention voted to leave such matters to others. This, no doubt, was partly due to an innate lack of interest in national politics, partly due to a sense of helplessness before the power of the state and the army and partly to the belief, supported by the apostle Paul, that anything savouring of violent action against the powers in being was forbidden to the Christian.

On the other hand it must be recognized that the Great Rebellion created a generation where Baptists, like others, were more aware perhaps than ever before that political action was possible for ordinary people. This was the first great modern disturbance of the traditional order. This was the period when, with other Englishmen, though only for a short time, they overthrew their medieval inheritance of monarchy, aristocracy and an established ecclesiastical order. In an era of revolution when first the king's power was wrested from him by parliament, then parliament's power was taken from them by the army, then a military dictatorship gave place to the old royal family once more, many men were forced to make up their minds about their own personal obedience or at least to think a little about national politics, who had never thought about such matters before.

But political convictions were not merely the product of the abrupt changes in the possession of power which were shaking the foundations of English society: Baptists and other sectaries could not help being deeply and personally involved politically. They had a vested interest in the kind of government which would guarantee a large measure of religious freedom such as Cromwell's religious policies provided. After all, they had in many cases the best of reasons for knowing that such freedom was unlikely to continue to be theirs if the episcopalians or the presbyterians regained power. Baptists then, tended to be politically concerned (when they took an interest in such matters at all) because not only did they frequently come from the poorer class of people who could for the first time glimpse the possibility of political power and influence for themselves but also because they wished for further reforms. These would include their freedom of worship and freedom from the financial exactions of a church from which they had conscientiously withdrawn. Hence there arose, in particular, the great matter of tithes - the taxes demanded by the authorities of church and state from time immemorial for the support of the clergy of the established church whether ruled from Rome or from Canterbury. During the period of the Commonwealth and the Protectorate the hardline episcopalians were replaced in the parishes by men who either tolerated or enthusiastically embraced Presbyterian or Independent views together with a very few who were, or were later to become, Baptists. These men, all those who staffed the English parishes, whatever their ecclesiastical views, became heirs of the traditional system of tithes.

The first full discussion of the question appears to have taken place during the Midland Association meeting at Moreton-in-the-Marsh, 24 October 1655. There it was agreed that no Baptist minister should be supported by tithes though some who were present thought that other support 'provided the maintenance be freely given' might be accepted. There was also unanimous agreement that no true minister could be allowed 'to go forth to preach by the magistrate's authority and to be maintained by him accordingly'. This was because only a gathered church, possessing the power of Christ himself, had that right. Nevertheless the messengers, perhaps conscious of differences among themselves did not take the matter further.

At the meeting, however, during the following March at Tetsworth, the messengers of the Abingdon Association took the whole issue much further. The payment of tithes they maintained to be wrong because it upheld the law now abrogated in Christ and because it upheld the ministry of a false church. True ministers, they argued, are to be supported by 'the voluntary contribution of those that are instructed by them'. They then went on to discuss three other ways in which Baptists might be tempted to support the parish system: by paying church rates, by burying their dead in churchyards and by sharing in christening feasts 'held in honour of the mock-baptism of infants'. All these, it was argued, should be rejected and the churches were advised to consider obtaining their own graveyards. Some members of the church at Wantage argued in response to the advice against paying tithes that they should pay on the grounds that these were demanded not as of divine right but as a matter of civil obedience. The messengers answered that this was to require disobedience to God and not even the civil power had the right to exact that.

When the Western Association met at Wells, 8-10 April 1656, the issue was looked at from the other side: should a minister accept any set maintenance from those who were not churchmembers? The messengers' judgment was apparently unanimous: ministers should not take such maintenance for five reasons. First, the Lord's people should support the Lord's work - if the church sending the minister forth could not wholly support him other churches should assist them. Secondly, formal stipends would tie ministers to fixed times and places. Thirdly, they would stop ministers from a clear witness against the parochial ministry. Fourthly, to take such stipends had the appearance of the sin of covetousness. Finally, acceptance of such support disobeyed Christ's command to give freely. Meeting at Bridgewater the following November the messengers recognized that some churches still allowed the taking of a set maintenance from the magistrate for preaching but only insisted that it was the duty of those who saw their way clear to bear testimony against it. At Tiverton in September 1657 the assembled company was asked for counsel as to what must be done when magistrates sought to tax the people for the maintenance of their ministers and to distrain in cases of non-payment. The messengers were not prepared to demand the heroic and answered:

> ... at least they ought to bear a public testimony against it as a soul oppressing and offending yoke and, if any have faith to expose themselves in sufferings by refusing utterly to pay through a real scruple in tenderness of conscience only towards God, we desire them to walk according to their faith and understanding uprightly whatever they may suffer from men, with meekness committing themselves to God, as into the hands of a faithful Creator.

It is clear that the Calvinistic Baptists rejected tithes and church rates not merely because they were costly to people already supporting their own ministers but because such exactions supported what they believed to be an altogether false ecclesiastical system. The great majority of them believed that their ministers should not be supported by such a system. Two men came under considerable pressure on this issue during the 1650s. One of them was John Miles in South Wales and the other was Richard Harrison who in 1657 was minister of the church at Hereford. William Kiffin and several other leaders of the churches met at

Devizes in Wiltshire in July 1657 to discuss Harrison's case and give counsel upon it. Their position was clear: it was the task of the church to see its minister and his family were 'sufficiently and comfortably supplied' and, if they could not, to secure assistance from other churches. No minister should allow his salary to be augmented by state support and, should he persist in doing so, his church should discipline him to the point, if necessary, of excommunication. Whether their advice was taken is unknown.[29]

But association meetings were not merely taken up with matters of discipline even though, of necessity for a generation concerned with searching out the true scriptural pattern for the lives of members and churches, such matters had to be given a considerable attention. In fact, prayer played a large part in these gatherings and, on more than one occasion, they were obviously deeply moving. From the Wells meeting in April 1656 the gathered messengers of the Western Association reported: 'We have seen the Lord exalted and his train filling the Temple. We have in some measure been embracing our dear Jesus who hath made us even sick with love and overcome with longings for that day of glory when we shall appear with him and be made like him and shall for ever be with him not only beholding but enjoying glory. Oh, if the crumbs be so sweet as to make us rejoice with joy unspeakable and full of glory what will it be when faith and hope will stand aside and we sit down at table to enjoy fulness of glory.[30]

With the death of Oliver Cromwell, 3 September 1658, the golden days began to draw to an end for the Baptists and other sectaries. The Western Association's letter reporting the discussions and decisions taken at Bridgwater in October 1659 betrayed no consciousness of this: their chief concern seemed to be that the churches would hasten to the appointment of proper officers to carry on the work of the ministry among them. Nevertheless, a spirit of foreboding was reflected in the letter sent from the Abingdon Association's meeting at Tetsworth 24-25 April 1660 and, by that stage, their churches seemed only too well aware that storm clouds were gathering.[31] While Richard Cromwell's succession had at first seemed to take place peaceably enough it soon became clear that the pressures Oliver had been strong enough to resist would be too great for his son. Richard withdrew into private life in May 1659. After much political and military manoevring a Parliament met on 25 April 1660 which was clearly Presbyterian and Royalist in its sympathies. It quickly accepted the Declaration made by Charles II from Breda promising, among other matters, liberty of conscience in matters of religion, as a basis for his restoration. All was, of course, to be dependent upon confirmation by Parliament later. The Baptists had good cause to be apprehensive.

3.
The End of the Great Persecution 1660–1688

The particular form in which liberty of conscience was promised from Breda in April 1660 was somewhat ambiguous: 'we do declare a liberty to tender consciences, and that no man shall be disquieted, or called into question, for differences of opinion in matters of religion which do not disturb the general peace of the kingdom'.[1] Whether Charles II was sincere in this and genuinely desired toleration for those who remained outside the established Church, as some have claimed, or whether he was entirely dishonest, as others have argued, will never be known for there is evidence to support both views. What very soon became clear, however, was that since 'differences of opinion in matters of religion' were judged by a majority in parliament from 1661 onwards inevitably to 'disturb the general peace of the kingdom' dissenters of any kind, whether Protestants or Roman Catholics, could only expect serious trouble. There can also be little doubt that the king, and perhaps most of his chief advisers, were taken by surprise at the violence of the reaction, especially among the gentry who were to supply the magistracy locally and members of parliament, against those who had dominated or who had profited from the state of church affairs in England during much of the previous twenty years.

With hindsight some of the major causes of this reaction are easy enough to recognize though it is clear that they operated with different force for different people at different times. First, recent research has shown that a fierce loyalty to the more high church party in the Church of England had been nurtured by ministers committed to the churchmanship represented by Archbishop Laud and his disciples who had acted as chaplains to many gentry families during the 1640s and 1650s. Secondly, there was a strong conviction, held by many, both high and low in churchmanship and high and low in society, that there should be one church and one church only in the land to provide cement and stability for a deeply disturbed society. Thirdly there was the belief, sometimes explicit but normally implicit, that a hierarchical church fitted most properly with a hierarchical society. Fourthly and more negatively, there was a sense abroad that the multiplicity of sects which had developed in the 1640s and 1650s had contributed to the unsettlement of society because so many of them seemed also to promote political instability. Fifthly, it was felt that loyalty to the restored episcopal establishment best expressed loyalty to the restored monarchy and the general sense that Englishmen had had enough of revolutions. Finally, closely linked with the others and perhaps most fundamentally so for many of the gentry, was the sense that when they had joined 'in challenging the ancient structures of royal and episcopal authority, they had unwittingly struck at the foundations of their own power'.[2] Obviously these various factors were closely interwoven with the emotions as well as the thought processes of many Englishmen, but the one undoubted fact is that together they coalesced into a very powerful reactionary force in parliament.

The Persecution begins

The immediate consequences of such feelings when released by the king's return (he disembarked at Dover on 25 May 1660) were illustrated by Henry Jessey's booklet, *The Lord's Loud Call to England* whose introduction was signed on 12 August. In it there were plenty of indications of how the general attitude towards Congregationalists and Baptists in particular had already changed from that of tolerance to that of outright hostility. Among the events which Jessey mentioned were the havoc made by a mob of the meeting place of William Kiffin's London congregation; the imprisonment of the Welsh evangelist, Vavasor Powell, without trial, together with the plunder of his friends' homes by soldiers; the July petition to the king by a number of Lincolnshire General Baptists for protection (their local magistrates had significantly refused to help) against those who stoned them as they came together for worship; the congregationalist ministers and their people in Gloucestershire who had been beaten up and their homes looted by royalist enthusiasts. The Gloucestershire troubles appear to have dated from March, that is, from even before the King's return. Then there was a letter, from Reading gaol, from some of the leaders of the Baptist Abingdon association, where they had been thrown into prison for refusing to take oaths they thought unlawful. For the encouragement of their readers the Reading group reported that, nevertheless, the congregations from which they had come 'are exceedingly cheerful, and a very lively spirit of faith and prayer is amongst them and their meetings rather increaseth than otherwise'.[3]

In order partly to clear themselves of suspicions that they were planning a violent rising in London and partly to show that their beliefs belonged to the Christian mainstream, some General Baptists published *A brief Confession or Declaration of Faith* in March 1660. Its forty signatories, of whom half seem to have come from London and Kent and most of the rest from the home counties, did not represent the whole General Baptist community at the time but their Confession was, gradually, to be accepted as the standard for virtually all General Baptists after modifications in 1663, 1678 and 1700.

In article XII they asserted that 'it is the duty of all such who are believers Baptized to draw nigh unto God in submission to that principle of Christ's doctrine, to wit, prayer and laying on of hands, that they may receive the promise of the Holy Spirit'. Evidently by this time the laying on of hands at baptism had become normal practice:

the chief difference between General Baptists seems to have been whether it should be demanded invariably. Later, in article XXIV, they asserted their belief that it was God's will 'that all men should have the free liberty of their own consciences in matters of religion, or worship, without the least oppression or persecution, as simply upon that account'. Naturally they were also careful to express their belief that civil magistrates had a part to play in enforcing 'just and wholesome' laws but they insisted that if those same civil magistrates imposed things in the area of religion which the signatories believed in conscience they could not obey they must 'obey God rather than men, *Acts* 5.29' and submit to the consequences without attempting to defend themselves. All too soon their convictions were to be thoroughly tested on this last point.

Once the king had returned the balance of power within the Church of England shifted almost at once: for, immediately, decisions had to be taken and appointments made and, naturally, these were very largely made according to the counsel of the Anglicans linked most closely with the court. These men regarded both the Presbyterians and the whole spectrum of sectaries to their left as not only hostile to the true interests of the Church of England but as potentially revolutionary. It was the combination of earlier ecclesiastical changes and political revolution represented by those who dissented from the episcopalian way as seen by the new masters of the Church of England which gave a sharper edge, from the point of view of the establishment, to the acts of persecution which were to follow.

A measure of justification for the belief that dissent meant disloyalty and revolution was given in early January 1661 by the rising in London led by Thomas Venner. Some fifty of his followers drove back a force of militia sent against them. It was not until 9 January that they encountered some regular soldiers and, after a fierce engagement,

Venner's supporters were either killed, captured or scattered. Their sympathies seem to have been Fifth Monarchist but their practical intentions were vague. Once calm had been restored in the capital Venner and twelve others were executed and their meeting house was destroyed. Venner had not been a Baptist but the anxious authorities carried out a wave of arrests including Baptists, Congregationalists and Quakers to ensure there would be no more trouble.

The day after Thomas Venner's arrest the government made a first move against the 'anabaptists, quakers and other sectaries' warning them not to meet at 'unusual hours, nor in great numbers' nor leave their homes for 'any spiritual exercise, or serving of God after their own way, but that they do the same in their own parish'.[4] This somewhat ambiguously worded proclamation was to be enforced by magistrates according to the laws provided against riotous and unlawful assemblies. With this the first official blow was struck against the left wing of Dissent. By the end of the month a group of both Calvinistic and General Baptists, led by William Kiffin and Henry Denne, had publicly repudiated Venner and his people. They not only pointed out that, as far as they knew, all but one of his followers had believed in infant baptism but, furthermore, that Venner's supporters had bitterly attacked the Baptists for their faith in and practice of submission to the civil power. They also argued that it was unjust to impute the failings of the continental Anabaptists in another time and in another place to the English Baptists then.[5]

Henry Adis, an upholsterer living near Covent Garden and a General Baptist pastor, had been imprisoned with two of his churchmembers as the result of the arrests which followed the Venner affair. He complained that the meetings of his church had been upset by 'rude and debauched soldiers' accompanied by a mob in spite of his assertion that he owned Charles II as lawful king. This, he explained, meant that even if the king's commands went against his conscience he would patiently suffer the consequences of disobedience without any violent resistance. Sufferings, he reported, were already being experienced by some other congregations in the city: in one a man had been so injured that he was likely to lose the use of his hand; in another the soldiers and the mob had drunk up the communion wine; in another they had broken up the communion table and in yet another they had beaten up the worshippers. Not content with this, after Venner's insurrection, when houses were searched the searchers forced their way in and took away whatever they pleased. He begged the king that in future when no offence had been proved to be committed arrests should be non-violent.[6]

While there can be little doubt that the people who suffered most from the casual and illegal violence of soldiers and others were those on the left-wing of Dissent the government's own first formal effort to bring all the Protestant dissenting groups into line was the Corporation Act which received the royal assent, after a rather difficult passage through Parliament, in December 1661. Obviously, from the authorities' point of view, there was every need to ensure that local government was firmly in the hands of royalists as soon as possible. The people to whom the Act referred were 'mayors, aldermen, recorders, bailiffs, town clerks, common councilmen and other persons bearing any office or offices of magistracy, or places or trusts or other employment relating to or concerning the government of the said respective cities, corporations and boroughs and cinque ports and their members and other port towns'. They must now take the Oaths of Allegiance and Supremacy; then they must assert that they 'do declare and believe that it is not lawful upon any pretence whatsoever to take arms against the king' and make a formal disavowal of the Solemn League and Covenant (1643) which had committed

England to a presbyterian church settlement. Anyone who refused to make these oaths and declarations was regarded as removed from office from that moment. Over and above all this there were royal commissioners appointed under the act who could even dismiss any of those who had taken the necessary oaths and made the necessary declarations if the commissioners thought it wise. Furthermore, henceforward no appointment or election would be counted valid unless the appointee had 'within one year next before such election or choice taken the sacrament of the Lord's Supper according to the rites of the Church of England.'[7] The provisions of this act would be very difficult for the great majority of Baptists to meet: it would be one thing to deny the rightness of the earlier presbyterian church settlement but quite another to affirm the king's supremacy in matters ecclesiastical. Similarly, it would be one thing to swear allegiance to the king (an oath directed against the papists) and another to take the Lord's Supper in their parish church to qualify for office. One did not have to be very extreme in one's dissent to be uneasy about this last requirement or to know how vulnerable one would be to accusations of blasphemy as well as disloyalty to Baptist witness.

Earlier that autumn there had been the pathetic and apparently grossly unjust trial and execution of John James. James had been the pastor of a Seventh-day church in Bulstake Alley, Whitechapel. He was interrupted in the midst of preaching and brought before a magistrate on a charge of speaking treason against the king. His congregation unitedly denied his guilt but under interrogation James admitted to Fifth Monarchy beliefs. Although he condemned Venner's rising and claimed that far from praising Cromwell, he personally had suffered from him, he was judged guilty and was executed at Tyburn on 26 November, in spite of a petition by his wife to the king for mercy.[8] Baptists were to continue to suffer for the identification made both in the public mind and, apparently, by the authorities with the continental anabaptists of Munster over a century before. Although it might reasonably be thought that there were weapons enough already in the legislative armoury to enable the government to deal with dissenters feared to be potential traitors, those newly restored to power did not think so. The matter did not rest there because it seems clear that the authorities did not believe that they would really be safe until there was one church in the land.

A measure of paranoia in government circles was perhaps only to be expected after the events of the previous twenty years but the authorities were far too quick to believe rumours and odd witnesses to plots. On the other hand, Baptist apologists then and since have tended to forget that there was undeniable evidence of the involvement of individuals linked with the Baptist community in more than one attempt to upset the restored Stuart regime. In the Act of Oblivion (1660) those responsible for trying, sentencing and executing Charles I had been omitted from the general pardon. Among the regicides who were executed were at least two who were known not merely to have shared Baptist views but to have been closely linked with the Baptist community, John Carew and Thomas Harrison. Daniel Axtell, whose regiment provided the guard during the trial and who had been a member of Kiffin's congregation as early as 1649, was also put to death.

Both the Venner rising and the account of John James's trial make it clear that any kind of Fifth Monarchy views were regarded as politically dangerous and that the authorities did not attempt to make any distinction between those who were relatively harmless Bible students and those who were potential or actual revolutionaries. It is therefore the more significant for official views of the Baptist community as a whole that a number of men who had been active among them in the 1640s and 1650s were identified as linked with Fifth Monarchy views by government agents after the restoration. These included William Allen, Henry Jessey, Nathaniel Strange, Thomas Tillam and John Vernon, together with a number of less well known figures. If to these are added Paul Hobson, one of the outstanding leaders of the earlier period, who was deeply involved in the incompetent and abortive plottings in Yorkshire and the north in 1663[9], some government unease with Baptists over and beyond the associations of the name 'anabaptist' might seem justified. Nor did the 1663 plot mark the end of Baptist involvement in revolutionary plotting.

The Great Ejectment and Persecution to 1672

Whatever the rights and wrongs of government suspicions of some left-wing protestants a gradual framework of legislation from the Corporation Act onwards was built up to protect an Anglican monopoly. From the parliamentary elections in 1661 there had emerged a rocklike royalist and Anglican majority which met for the first time on 8 May 1661. In April a series of meetings between church leaders at the Savoy had begun but by its close in July it was clear that it had had no success in healing the divisions between Anglicans and Presbyterians, much less with those Protestants further to the left: the Independents, the Baptists and the Quakers. Later in the year the Anglicans prepared a revision of the *Book of Common Prayer* which was accepted by both Houses of Parliament in April 1662. Now, as David Ogg remarked, 'the liturgy of the Church of England was amended and restored, it remained only to establish the monopoly of a state church on the basis of penal legislation'.[10]

While the Act of Uniformity, which received the royal assent on 19 May 1662, was marginal for most Baptists in its immediate, personal impact at the time, it was nevertheless, in the longer run, extremely important for them. The Act required that all ministers should have received episcopal ordination and that, on pain of deprivation of every ecclesiastical office held, each minister must, upon some Lord's Day before the feast of St Bartholomew (24 August) publicly assert his 'unfeigned assent and consent to all and everything contained and prescribed in and by ... the Book of Common Prayer'. Furthermore he must also declare 'that it is not lawful under any pretence whatsoever, to take up arms against the king' and that the Solemn League and Covenant was 'an unlawful oath' whose promises neither he nor anyone else had any obligation to keep'.[11] Some seven hundred ministers whose appointments had been made during the interregnum had already been compelled to vacate their livings by various kinds of pressure before this. Now another thousand or more ministers were to abandon their positions because they were unable to make the declarations required. Because, as has been seen, on principle the vast majority of Baptists, whether Arminian, Calvinistic or Seventh Day rejected the whole concept of an established Church and its methods of appointment and payment even if they were qualified to receive them, as for example was Hanserd Knollys, formerly a Church of England minister himself, only a tiny minority of their men was affected. In England these included John Tombes, perhaps the most learned of all the Baptists, vicar of Leominster; Henry Jessey, who held a lectureship at St George's Church, Southwark; Paul Hobson who was chaplain at Eton College; John Skinner who was rector of Weston-under-Penyard with Hope Mansell, Herefordshire; Richard Harrison who led the gathered church at Netherton and William Kaye, rector of Stokesley, Yorkshire. These six can reasonably, though not in every case with total certainty, be regarded as Baptists who had held paid appointments within the English church establishment of the 1650s, who had led gathered congregations where believer's baptism was taught and who lost their posts during the period 1660-62. Ejections of similar men in Wales included John Miles and Vavasor Powell.

Others who were ejected in England certainly became Baptists later: Richard Adams was one who may have held these convictions before 1662. All these men, with the possible exception of Paul Hobson whose relationship to the Calvinistic Baptist community to which he had earlier belonged was by the 1660s somewhat uncertain, seem to have been Calvinists at this time and to have practised open communion and open membership: there was little to differentite them from the main body of Independents or Congregationalists.[12]

A G Matthews reckoned that a total of 1,760 ministers were ultimately ejected. By local initiative, as the result of the Act for Confirming and Restoring of Ministers (29 December 1660) - those not "confirmed" included men who had "given judgment" against infant baptism - and by the 1662 Act of Uniformity.[13] The indirect consequences for Baptists, as has been pointed out,[14] were very considerable indeed. First, when so many men and their congregations left the established Church it meant that Dissent, as a body, was now more likely to survive than if it had been reduced to a few Independents, the Baptists and the Quakers. Secondly, a number of the ejected ministers and their people came to reconsider the whole question of believer's baptism and this led not merely to the ministers coming to change their convictions in the matter but also to the foundation of a number of new Baptist churches during the persecution time.

However, Baptist congregations could be immediately vulnerable, for the Act of Uniformity laid down that the reading of the Prayer Book services was "to the intent that every person within this realm may certainly know the rule to which he is to conform in public worship". This emphasized that the government envisaged one church with no toleration of alternative forms of worship even if these and the ministers responsible for them were to be supported from the pocket of any who dissented. For example at Abingdon, Berkshire, the records of the borough sessions for the period between 1662 and the first Conventicle Act of 1664 contain frequent reports of proceedings taken against people of the town either for non-attendance at their parish church or 'for maliciously and seditiously assembling in unlawful conventicles under pretence of religion'. Among others in trouble on these counts was Thomasina Pendarves, widow of the former Baptist pastor in the town.[15]

When the mayor of Bristol sent for the Broadmead pastor, Thomas Ewins, in October 1663 and attempted to forbid him to preach Ewins replied that 'he must discharge his duty towards the Lord and therefore in that thing he durst not obey him'. Ewins was imprisoned for nearly a year until a small fine was paid on his behalf.[16] A very different case arose at Aylesbury in Buckinghamshire when some General Baptists were arrested for holding an illegal conventicle. The legislation under which the case was dealt with was not the first Conventicle Act recently passed but one from Queen Elizabeth's time aimed at both Roman Catholics and Separatists.[17] Twelve General Baptists, ten men and two women, had been arrested and convicted for conventicling. When they were brought before the quarter sessions for sentencing they were required either to conform to the Church of England or to go into exile as the Elizabethan law required. If they refused either to conform or leave the country, sentence of death would be passed on them. They were given until the afternoon to decide what they would do. In the afternoon they announced that they could do neither and must therefore throw themselves on the mercy of court. Sentence of death was then passed upon them, and their possessions were seized. One man, moved by his wife's tears, took the oaths the court required under this threat but afterwards repented and returned to prison. Fortunately, Thomas Monk, a son of one of the prisoners, rode to London to seek help from William Kiffin. Kiffin took him to see the Lord Chancellor, Edward Hyde, to request the king's intervention. Charles claimed to be astonished by their story and by the possibility that such a law remained on the statute book; at all events he granted an immediate reprieve and the prisoners were saved. However, the case provided evidence that there was already plenty of legal provision for the persecution of dissent![18]

In May 1664 Parliament, apparently on the basis of the threat which the Yorkshire plot of the autumn before had offered to the tranquillity of the kingdom, passed the first Conventicle Act. This made it illegal for more than five persons over the age of sixteen (apart from members of the same household) to assemble together for worship except according to the rites of the *Book of Common Prayer*. Disobedience would result in either a fine of £5 or three months imprisonment for the first offence and a fine of £10 or six months imprisonment for the second offence; for a third offence those convicted would go to the assizes where they could be sentenced to either £100 or seven years transportation.[19] It seems likely that the implementation of this last penalty was dropped partly because of the difficulty of persuading the colonies to accept such convicts.[20]

Persecution was patchy depending very much on local personalities and relationships: in some places it is amazing that congregations survived at all but it is clear that neither in the central government nor in local circumstances was there a consistent will to root out all Dissent. Nevertheless, life could be made very difficult for those who did not conform. One method which did not need the assistance of the Conventicle Act was the age-old process of excommunication. On 13 October 1669 a decree of excommunication against Consolation Fox, one of the leaders of the Abingdon Baptists and a former Cromwellian officer, together with a number of others, was published. Obviously the spiritual implications of being cast out from a church which they already considered a false one would not greatly concern such people. However, there were other consequences in everyday life: theoretically, at least, they would suffer a boycott in business affairs and an inability to act in legal matters but, above all, there was the threat of imprisonment until submission. When Fox and four other Baptists had the decree reaffirmed in December they were sufficiently intimidated to make their submission in the archdeacon's court in Oxford and enter into a bond of £20 each 'to obey the laws and stand by the commands of the English Church'. Quite soon he was recorded as having relapsed and having become a frequenter of conventicles again. Nevertheless, the Anglicans kept the machinery of excommunication in operation to bring pressure to bear upon the Abingdon Dissenters on and off through most of the remainder of the persecution time.[21]

Amazingly, somehow, the life of the congregations was carried on. The discipline of the churches was maintained: at its best it meant that kind of care for one another whereby the members held each other up to what they believed to be a high and holy obedience to Christ. In 1663 in the General Baptist congregation at Warboys, Huntingdonshire, John Christmas, 'for not loving Ann his wife as he ought and for speaking hateful and despising words against her ... after sundry admonitions was withdrawn from'. He afterwards sent for Ann and promised a new start. When she had returned he asked to be received by the church once more and 'was joined in fellowship again'. Mary Flower, however, was cast out 'for marrying with one not in the fellowship of the Gospel'. This insistence that marriage should be between Christians, and probably between General Baptists at that, was reflected in discussions which took place at an assembly (it is not known how representative this was) held in London on 4 May 1668. The implications of the fragmentary report are not wholly clear but it was agreed 'that the general estimation that the Scriptures make of a Believer and Unbeliever is, that he is or is not a member of a visible Church of Christ'. So to marry one who was, in these terms, an unbeliever was to commit sin.22

The broad outlines of the shape of Baptist theological writing during the period can be discerned from W T Whitley's Bibliography.[23] The figures for writings of this kind attributed to Baptists during the period 1660-1688 (which include John Bunyan's but omit John Milton's) must be somewhat arbitrary because the publications concerned would not in every case fall into one simple category. However, if the general classification were allowed to include deliberately devotional writings, memorials for dead friends and such pieces as Hanserd Knollys' linguistic studies as well as theological debates including that, largely among the General Baptists, on the laying on of hands, it would amount to 142. The remainder, another 136, were controversial writings directed largely outside the various Baptist groupings. These include an outburst (32) of declarations, confessions and petitions largely from the first year or so of the restoration; a debate about the lawfulness of taking oaths (9) from the same period; a further group (24) dealing with questions concerning toleration and relationships with the established Church; a number (28) arguing about believer's baptism and, in some cases, what would now be termed 'open membership'; two small groups debating the Seventh Day Sabbath (9); and the errors of the Church of Rome (7). Finally, there was the regular production (partly from the middle 1670s as the result of a major debate) throughout the period (27) of controversial writings against the Quakers. It is clear that both General and Particular Baptists felt the strength of the Quaker case and its influence upon some of their rank and file. It is also worth noting that throughout this difficult period it was possible to ensure that a trickle of books was published even if that only meant an average of ten a year.

After the first spurt of persecution encouraged by the Conventicles Act of 1664 there seems to have been a slow but marked easing of the general situation of Dissent during the later 1660s. This[24] has been attributed to various factors including the devotion shown by their ministers during the Plague of London in 1665 and its aftermath and the government's unwillingness to stir the Calvinists at home to desperation when engaged in war during 1665-7 with their close friends in Holland. No doubt, too, for many the hostility and distrust of Dissent as a whole which had been felt during the early months and years of the restoration was slowly dying away.

After the fall of Clarendon in 1667 and as the statutory limits (three years and one parliamentary session) of the Conventicles Act began to run out, some members of the government with the more moderate Anglicans sought a new measure of comprehension, for the Presbyterians at least, within the established Church. However, those about the king who apparently genuinely favoured such changes were routed by the rigid Anglicans of the House of Commons led from the Lords by the Archbishop of Canterbury, Gilbert Sheldon. In the ensuing reaction, in spite of the efforts of more moderate parliamentarians, a much more severe Conventicles Act became law in 1670.

Unlike the former act this empowered one rather than two justices of the peace, even without specific evidence but only on the basis of 'notorious evidence and circumstance' leading him to believe a conventicle had been held, to convict and penalize. Each of those present could be fined five shillings for a first offence and ten shillings thereafter. If necessary the fine could be secured 'by distress and sale of the offender's goods and chattels' or, if he were too poor, from another convicted with him, provided the wealthier man were not fined in total more than a sum of £10. The minister present, if convicted, would be fined £20 for a first offence and £40 for any thereafter, as would anyone providing the meetingplace for the conventicle. Minor officials knowing of and not acting upon information concerning these illegal meetings would be fined £5 and a

THOMAS HARDCASTLE

Reproduced by permission of
Mrs J. A. L. Hardcastle

justice of the peace £100.[25] There was one more provision which added a further edge to the effectiveness of the act: the fines were to be divided equally between the king, the poor and the informer upon whose information a successful prosecution took place. Not only were informers thereby 'encouraged to ruin their nonconformist neighbours but were enabled to compel the officers of the law to act as their accomplices'.[26] The impact of such fines for minister and congregations can be judged both from the salary it was proposed to raise for the Broadmead pastor, Thomas Hardcastle, in 1671 and from the sum promised by members towards it. It was decided that he should be paid £80 per year to provide for him and his family comfortably. Apart from two larger individual pledges of £5 and £6 respectively promises ranged from 6 shillings to £4 per year.[27]

The Declaration of Indulgence and the Years before the Popish Plot

While the Dissenters suffered under the vicious provisions of the second Convencticles Act the king, with his ministers, was planning a Declaration of Indulgence. When this was eventually made, 15 March 1672, it suspended the penal laws against both Protestant Dissenters and Roman Catholics. It was received with very mixed feelings by the Dissenters. First, whatever the bitterness of the House of Commons to them at that time, the Dissenters themselves were very unwilling to acknowledge that the king possessed any large extra-parliamentary powers. Secondly, they shared the suspicion of many Anglicans that the easement of the position of the Roman Catholics might be a first step toward setting that communion on the road to capturing the position of the established Church. As Professor J R Jones has pointed out, no-one was likely to be deceived by the fact that the Indulgence allowed the Dissenters to meet publicly and the Catholics only privately: this was hardly a loss to the Catholics who knew that public worship 'would merely inflame popular anti-catholic prejudices'.[28] If the Roman Catholics did become supreme there was good reason to fear the position of Dissent would be more difficult than it had ever been under Anglican persecution. Thirdly, the more cynical suspected that the registration of teachers and meeting-places under the Indulgence would merely provide assistance for the authorities at the next turn of the wheel of persecution politics.

Nevertheless, with whatever misgivings, after twelve years of intermittent and often costly persecution, many Baptists joined the Presbyterians and the Independents who accepted the opportunity the Declaration of Indulgence offered. Others, like the Quakers, from the conviction that the king had no right to take away, still profited from the period during which the Indulgence was effective by going about their meetings without the same likelihood of prosecution even though they did not seek licences. Unfortunately, however, the king needed money and so, in February 1673, parliament had to be recalled. They quickly made it clear that unless the king withdrew the Declaration there would be no supplies so, on 8 March, he capitulated. From now onwards Charles II seems to have judged that it would best serve his purpose to make a firm alliance with the Anglicans and this he did.

After the withdrawal of the Declaration there was for some time doubt about the legal situation. While the licences no longer strictly provided any protection, legal magistrates were undecided how to act. Most nonconformist congregations continued to meet as if nothing had happened. The Broadmead, Bristol, church's experience was probably not untypical: it was not until 1674 that the processes of persecution set up by the second Conventicles Act were once more brought into use. Even in this case the change was apparently due to the appointment of a new rigorist bishop who had said 'he would not leave the track of a meeting in

Bristol, but would make us all come to church (as he called it)'. Unfortunately he found aid and support from the new mayor and a lawyer churchwarden from St James's parish in which both the Broadmead church and the closed membership congregation led by Andrew Gifford were accustomed to meet.[29]

There were four other congregations of Dissenters in Bristol at this time in addition to the Quakers who were not listed by the Broadmead records: a large Presbyterian congregation, two Independent churches and a church of sixty to eighty members led by a man called Kitchen who had been a captain in the army in earlier days. This General Baptist group represented one of the successes of the persecution since, sometime between 1675 and 1681, it dissolved.[30]

The pattern of persecution for the protestant Dissenters of Bristol was a simple one after 1672. First there was a period of uncertainty, then there was the royal proclamation of February 1675 which announced that all licences acquired under the Declaration of Indulgence were now void. Next there was an immediate twelve-month of sharp and persistent persecution as the Dissenters' local enemies moved in on them on the basis of the second Conventicles Act which they now once more enforced. The second period of persecution, after four and a half quiet years, lasted from the summer of 1680 until the death of Charles II.

By early March 1675 all four ministers of the larger congregations were in prison - Andrew Gifford of the closed membership Pithay church was the last to be arrested on 1 March. Meetings of representatives of the four churches were held to attempt to work out a common policy about "how to carry on our meetings ... and edify one another now our pastors were gone". The Presbyterians, with their emphasis upon a learned ministry, were in the greatest difficulty and were also most cautious about co-operation though it was eventually agreed in July that there should be a joint quarterly prayer meeting at which one of the pastors, if he were not in gaol, should speak each time. The persecution lasted a twelve month and for virtually all of it Hardcastle suffered some kind of imprisonment even if it were only house arrest. The church did not feel able to have the Lord's Supper without their minister to preside and so for eight months they were without. Very little is said directly in these records about the general impact of the persecution upon their church but a rare glimpse is given in the remark (presumably by Edward Terrill their first historian) that their congregation 'had grown very poor and lean through fines, imprisonment and constant worrying of us every day'. Terrill knew this better than most since he had taken more than his fair share of the sufferings which had been imposed upon them.[31]

In the quiet years there were a number of attempts to return to normality. On 26 October 1676 the Broadmead congregation decided to ask five of the London Baptist leaders, who were down in the Trowbridge district attempting to settle a doctrinal issue raised by Thomas Collier, to ordain Thomas Hardcastle. They were told, however, that this would be impossible since the ministers concerned had to return at once to London "because of great personal concerns at home". Of this group the most senior was William Kiffin who had himself originally encouraged Hardcastle to accept Broadmead's invitation. However, one of his companions, James Fitten, now pastor of the congregation once led by Henry Jessey, was unlikely to be comfortable about sharing in such a service. Even if Kiffin, as seems likely on this occasion, could overcome his "closed membership" scruples, Hardcastle had originally been a member of Fitten's church and had moved to the Broadmead pastorate in defiance of a decision of theirs inviting him to become their pastor. In fact, they continued to consider him one of their members. Another step taken by the Bristol Baptists towards establishing themselves and freeing themselves from Anglican power to allow or deny them burial rights was for the two congregations, Broadmead and Andrew Gifford's Pithay church, to obtain a graveyard which they could share.[32]

Abraham Cheare, who was pastor of the Calvinistic Baptist Church at Plymouth, may be taken as a not untypical pastor of the period. He seems to have been imprisoned for the greater part of the time after the restoration down to his death in 1668. He was a native of Plymouth who had been employed in the cloth trade as a fuller and had not been involved in the Civil War at all. However, he had been not only pastor of the Plymouth Baptists during the 1650s but had also been linked with their nationwide association organisation. He was imprisoned for three years at Exeter and then for a somewhat shorter period on Drake's Island in Plymouth Sound where he died after some months of illness in 1668. After his death some letters of his were published in a volume over his name entitled *Words in Season* (1668).[33]

In the letters he reflected a very clear theology of suffering under persecution and his concern for growth in holiness among his correspondents. In August 1663 he wrote to a friend recently released from prison, of how important it was 'to get the heart established with grace, drawn into a more substantial and experimental communion with Jesus Christ' and asserted that those who would seek such a deeper experience 'may have more advantage from the retirement of a nasty prison, than ... from being left to walk in a large place'. In line with this he had written to another friend in the previous September to answer a question about whether congregations should continue to meet during a time of persecution. Cheare insisted that the question was not whether there were grounds for continuing to meet but whether there could be any justification, having taken reasonable care to avoid arrest, for <u>not</u> meeting. Hence, in July 1664, he could write to a friend who had recently been arrested at a meeting for worship telling him of his 'real opportunity to exalt Jesus Christ in suffering for his name's sake'.

On the other hand Cheare was very fully aware that many people had been deeply disturbed by the onset of persecution and some had fallen away: in one letter he had a picture of them like a fleet of merchantmen 'who set out of their port beautifully equipped, laden, trimmed, in consortship' who met a storm: some hastened to their home port 'with design to adventure such storms no more'; some were utterly wrecked and castaway; some anchored where they were and wished for the storm to abate. Only a few pressed on to the port for which they had set out in obedience to their Owner's desires. Yet in the same letter Cheare, who was not a boastful man, could say of his own case, after more than five years imprisonment, 'I have never yet seen the least reason and (I praise Christ my Lord) never been under an hour's temptation, to relinquish or repent of my testimony in word or deed to any one persecuted truth of Christ for which I suffer'. It was this kind of spirit which was to bring many of the Baptists, together with many more of their dissenting brethren, to survive and sometimes triumph under their afflictions.[34]

In the late 1670s life was again for a while easier for the Dissenters and in 1678 the General Baptist publisher Francis Smith published as one volume a collection of the writings of the Lincolnshire General Baptist leader Thomas Grantham (1634-1692) entitled *Christianismus Primitivus*. The title indicated Grantham's intention to get behind the traditions of the Reformers, of the Medieval Church, of the Fathers, to the New Testament model. Among other matters he outlined what the General Baptists believed to be the true shape of the Christian ministry although they had come to some convictions which the Calvinists were a long way from sharing. The latter, tied perhaps more closely to the tradition which stemmed from Geneva, held doggedly, with the Independents and the Presbyterians, to the conviction of an absolute parity among all ministers. They believed that apostles had been given for the first planting of the Church and while persons of apostolic integrity and stature might be raised up from time to time in the history of the Church (Calvin himself suggested that Martin Luther might have been one of these) there was no continuing superior ministerial order which succeeded them. The General Baptists however, who yielded to none in their sense of the tragic part played in church history by a worldly, greedy and dictatorial episcopate, understood Scripture to teach that there was a continuing level of ministry above that of the pastor of an individual congregation.

There were, Grantham taught, three kinds of ministers given to the Church, "Messengers (or Apostles), Bishops (or Elders) and Deacons". The messengers share some of the functions of the apostles being itinerant ministers whose task is 'to plant Churches and to settle those in order who are as Sheep without a Shepherd'. The actual power and authority given to such ministers in their superintendency of the churches was left undefined but that Messengers, when elected by their brethren to that office, had some authority among the churches and the ministers was made clear. Similarly elders or pastors or bishops had a threefold responsibility, to oversee their congregations in terms of pastoral care and the teaching of sound doctrine, to feed them both with the exposition of the Scripture and with their own exemplification of the true Christian life and to govern them 'to exhort, reprove, rebuke with all authority; to bind and loose in conjunction with the Church of God'. While deacons primarily had the care of the needy in the congregations they might also preach if they had that gift.

Although none could be ordained who had not been elected by a majority of the congregation it was left clear that the voters would be the brethren not the sisters! Interestingly he did not use the word 'association' but did speak of general councils. Of these he said, 'we ought to consider with great respect what is concluded by a General Council of Christ's true Ministers, yet may lawfully doubt of what they deliver, unless they confirm it by the Word of the Lord'. The membership of such consultative bodies should be composed not only of messengers and elders but also of other brethren 'such (no doubt) as are judicious'.[35]

From Grantham's view that 'we ought to consider with great respect' the conclusions of church councils it seems likely that his view of the 'authority' of messengers was that of advisers whose counsel must be listened to with great respect and from which a church or minister should only differ with considerable caution.

Grantham had been born in Halton in Lincolnshire, had been baptized among the General Baptists in 1653 and had become pastor of a small church apparently drawing its members from Halton and the surrounding villages in 1656. Gradually, it seems, a number of small congregations of General Baptists were formed in south Lincolnshire. In 1662 he was imprisoned in Lincoln Gaol but his work continued after his release and he was made a messenger by 1678. Although he suffered several imprisonments during the remainder of the reign he remained active and removed to Norwich in 1685 or 1686 where he founded a new General Baptist congregation and from where in 1686 he founded another at Great Yarmouth. In 1688 Grantham baptized into membership 'after prayer to God, with laying on of hands for the promised Spirit' Richard Read and Susan Homes at Warboys. The churchbook described Grantham as 'an elder of the church' but it seems likely that he acted as a Messenger since the congregation's own elder (pastor) had died.It is to Thomas Grantham acting as a clerk that we are indebted for the record of the General Assembly in London held 21-3

May 1689. No assembly was held again in London until June 1691 and there an entry in the record noted that Nathaniel Foxwell was to be sent to assist Grantham in his work in Norwich. He died in January 1692 and was interred just inside the west door of St Stephen's parish church, Norwich, whose vicar, John Connould, was a close friend.

New Confessions of Faith

The easing of persecution in the late 1670s enabled the Calvinistic Baptists in 1677 as a community 'in London and the country' to publish their new Confession. This, which was to be republished by the 1689 Assembly after the Revolution, was quite explicitly a revision of the Savoy Confession of the Congregationalists which had itself been closely based at most points upon the Westminster Confession. The reason, said the Baptist writers, was not merely to explain their doctrinal position to other Christians and provide a teaching instrument for themselves but to show how much they had in common with the Congregationalists and the Presbyterians.

Of course, the Baptists took their own line on the 'ordinances' and, especially, on believer's baptism but they also had some important things to say about the ministry and about intercongregational association. A congregation, they said, could be considered 'completely organized' when they had both officers and members. Those officers were named elders and deacons. They were to be elected by the church because they were discerned to be 'fitted and gifted by the Holy Spirit' and they were to be set apart by fasting, prayer and the imposition of hands by 'the eldership of the church if there be any before constituted therein'. The Confession seems to assume that normally there would only be one elder and he would be termed the pastor. The pastor would be chiefly responsible for preaching but others gifted and fitted by the Spirit and approved and called by the Church would be expected to share this ministry. The pastor would also be responsible for prayer (it is not clear whether this would be only his own intercessions or his leading of the church's corporate worship) and 'to watch for the congregation's souls'. The church would be responsible for giving him 'a comfortable supply' sufficient to save him from being 'entangled in secular affairs' and also to enable him or them to exercise hospitality towards others. Meanwhile it was asserted that the churches 'ought to hold communion amongst themselves for their peace, increase of love and mutual edification'. However, the most characteristic statement of the needs and yet the limits of inter-congregational relationships was the following:

> In cases of difficulties and differences, either in point of doctrine or administration; wherein either the churches in general are concerned, or any one church, in their peace, union and edification ; or any member or members of any church are injured, in or by any proceedings in censures not agreeable to truth and order; it is according to the mind of Christ, that many churches holding communion together, do by their messengers meet to consider and give their advice in or about that matter in difference, to be reported to all the churches concerned; howbeit these messengers assembled, are not entrusted with any church power properly so called; or with any jurisdiction over the churches themselves, to exercise any censures over any churches, or persons, or to impose their determination on the churches or officers.[36]

In 1679 a group of General Baptists, led by Thomas Monk, the Messenger for Buckinghamshire and Hertfordshire, also put out a confession. This Orthodox Creed was intended, it said, to unite all Christians against Romanist errors in general and certain General Baptist Christological errors in particular. Monk had been one of those sentenced to death at Aylesbury in 1664 and had become a Messenger in 1670. He had decided with nearly all the leaders under his jurisdiction not to seek a licence under the Declaration of Indulgence and had steadily opposed what he believed to be the Sussex leader Matthew Caffyn's Christological heresy. Forty-four of the signatories of the Orthodox Creed came from Buckinghamshire and almost all the others from nearby. Unlike the earlier General Baptist Confession of 1660 and that of the Calvinists in 1677 which had represented most of their community, the Orthodox Confession was a party production whose wider influence it is difficult to assess. However it certainly provided a teaching tool for a number of the more traditionally orthodox General Baptists and, because questions of churchmanship were not at issue at the time between General Baptists, can be taken as a fair reflection of their ecclesiology. They believed that no-one could join the visible church of Christ without being baptized as a believer and that the several distinct congregations of believers made up the visible body of Christ. They also asserted that the marks of a true Church were that there the Word was truly preached and the sacraments (they apparently had no difficulty with the term) were rightly administered. However, it was made clear that this could not be so without the due adminstration of discipline to keep the church as pure as possible in both life and doctrine.

The officers of a true church they asserted to be three: 'Bishops or Messengers; and Elders, or Pastors; and deacons or overseers of the poor'. The Messengers should be elected by the churches: they would then have 'the government of those churches which had suffrage in their election and no other ordinarily'. Their ordination would be effected by other Messengers. When a pastor had been elected by a local congregation the Messenger for that district would be responsible for his ordination and he would have no authority outside his own congregation. The deacons would be appointed similarly and would be especially responsible for the finances of their own church. Evidently, however, it was now felt that the time for a tent-making ministry had passed for, like the Calvinists, it was agreed that the pastors (and messengers) should receive 'a sufficient and honourable maintenance of the people that chose them, answerable to the dignity of their places and charge committed to them, without which they cannot discharge their duty, as they ought to do, in studying to divide the Word of God aright'.

Alongside their teaching about a threefold order of ministry which inevitably implied a tighter intercongregational discipline than among the Calvinists was set a section headed 'Of general Councils, or Assemblies' as follows:

> General councils or assemblies, consisting of Bishops, Elders and Brethren, of the several churches of Christ, and being legally convened and met together out of all the churches, and the churches appearing there by their representatives, make but one church and have lawful right and suffrage in this general meeting or assembly to act in the name of Christ; it being of divine authority and is the best means under heaven to preserve unity, to prevent heresy, and superintendency among, or in any congregation whatsoever within its own limits or jurisdiction. And to such a meeting or assembly, appeals ought to be made, in case any injustice be done, or heresy and schism countenanced, in any particular congregation of Christ. And the decisive voice in such assemblies is the major part and such assemblies have lawful power to hear and determine as also to excommunicate.[37]

One congregation of General Baptists meeting in Amersham, Buckinghamshire, whose first members may originally have been linked with the Calvinists at Kensworth, was not, apparently, involved with those who published the Orthodox Creed. Nevertheless their records do give a valuable glimpse into congregational life in the provinces during the late 1670s. Their original nucleus seems to have been a house group led by David Jameson and reported in the Anglican records of 1669 but their church did not have its independent foundation until 1676.[38]

In August 1675, having become convinced that when believers were baptized it was essential also that hands should be laid upon them (as the General Baptist Brief Confession of 1660 had taught: 'that they may receive the promise of the Holy Spirit') the group asked the unnamed church to which they belonged to release them. They wanted this, they explained, because they could no longer remain members with a people who neither practiced the laying on of hands nor preached it as duty. Their church refused but, after some correspondence with them, the Amersham group approached John Griffith's General Baptists meeting at Dunning's Alley in London asking that they might receive the laying on of hands from them. In December Griffith himself came down to administer the rite.

They then began to formulate a basis, in several articles, for regulating their life together as an independent church. It was decided that they must limit fellowship at the Lord's Table to those who held the Six Principles of *Hebrews* 6.1-2 and to those who refused to take the oath of the royal supremacy and who would marry only 'in the Lord', that is, among those who held their position. They further agreed that visitors should only pray and preach among them if they could show a letter from their own church certifying that they were in good standing there; that no transfer of membership should be received without a similar assurance and that, within the Amersham church fellowship, should there be a difference between the officers and others, the final decision would lie with the congregation's judgment 'according to God's Word'. Finally it was agreed to follow what they believed to be the rule of the Word (presumably *Matthew* 18.15-17 but only *James* 5.20 is actually quoted) in dealing with broken relationships between any of the members.

On 12 February 1676 the company held a day of fasting and prayer 'committing themselves to the Lord and to each other by the will of God'. The following day, a Sunday, they 'sat down together as a Church of Christ' with David Jameson as their elder and with Edmund Rudrup as deacon. With the two officers included there were, in all, eight men and eleven women. Another woman, Mary Prat, probably the wife of one of the members, were baptized by the elder later that month 'and came under hands and subscribed the articles above said and sat down with us'. This was to be the threefold condition for becoming a member: believer's baptism, the laying on of hands and subscription to the articles governing the fellowship. In March the church held a day of prayer and fasting against 'the adversaries of truth' who had gaoled John Griffith in Newgate for a six month when he had refused to stop preaching. Their concern for the wider Baptist community was also shown the month after when a preacher from High Wycombe told them of a member with him whose house had just been burned down: the infant church sent the sum of thirteen shillings and eight pence to help. In June the first of several gifts (others were sent in October 1676, in September 1683, in December 1684 and January 1686) was sent for John Griffith and his fellow sufferers. From time to time the church was to arrange other days of prayer and fasting for both wider and more local and personal matters. Naturally, with their concern that marriages should take place within their branch of the Baptists, a marriage or two were recorded where the two engaged themselves 'to live together as man and wife and to perform all those duties (to the utmost of their power) as do relate to a husband and wife'. In August messengers were sent to Watford to introduce the Amersham church to the congregation there and to secure the transfer of one of their members. Apparently this was the Calvinistic Baptist church earlier linked with John Spilsbury in London and now, it seems, with Benjamin Keach with whom the two messengers from Amersham met on a further visit to Watford in September. It seems that Keach's change to the Calvinistic Baptists (if it had now taken place) was less important to the Amersham congregation than his commitment to the laying on of hands.

It is a little puzzling that this church seems to have stood rather aloof from the large Berkhamstead congregation of General Baptists led by Thomas Monk but it may be the explanation is given by the church's dealings with Thomas Trip. Trip, who proved to be a difficult member, had originally obtained a transfer from Berkhamstead to Amersham but, in a discussion over his move back to Berkhamstead at the Amersham church meeting in April 1679, it was hinted that he had left Monk's church believing it to be somewhat 'loose in judgment about the fourth principle' (ie laying on of hands). Formally Berkhamstead had not significantly changed its stance on the issue for the Orthodox Creed was quite clear on the matter in its article XXXII:

> Prayer, with imposition of hands by the bishop, or elder, on baptized believers, as such, for the reception of the holy promised Spirit of Christ, we believe is a principle of Christ's doctrine, and ought to be practised and submitted to by every baptized believer in order to receive the promised Spirit of the Father and the Son.

Meanwhile, on 27 December 1676, Rudrup and Thomas Charlsley were publicly set apart as deacons and their 'ordination' as it was termed in the churchbook, was conducted by the elder. At the same time another member, Nicholas Bennet, seems, without any recorded decision by the church, to have become largely (though not wholly, since the elder sometimes acted) responsible for the administration of baptism. Often the act of baptism and the act of laying on of hands seems to have been separated by a day or two and sometimes more. Whether the elder was alone responsible for the laying on of hands is not clear.

In the autumn of 1677 came the only mention of the church suffering directly from persecution itself. The activities of an informer threatened some of the members and in consequence Henry Pratt, a church member in whose home they had been accustomed to meet for some while past, asked that they agree to be responsible for any fines he should incur through the use of his house for illegal worship. This the church felt unable to do and, instead, quickly arranged for the building of a meetinghouse on part of a plot of land they had bought the previous year for a burial ground. The work was completed at a cost of £26.0.2 in time for the church to meet there on 30 December. Twenty-eight members of the fellowship subscribed £17.2.6 and Thomas Charsley undertook to bear the balance of the cost until the church could repay him. The first person recorded as being buried in the burial ground was a deacon of the Seventh Day church at Bledlow. Other Baptists came to want to use it and, while the churchbook meticulously registered the exact position of each body, in October 1678 it was decided to charge five shillings for the interment of each non-member.

At the end of July, Nicholas Bennet's brother Thomas, on a visit to Amersham, was convinced that he should be baptized with the laying on of hands. Afterwards, since he lived in London, he was commended to Benjamin Keach's church on Horslydown, Southwark. In December Nicholas himself married Elizabeth Alldwin from Watford who was received into membership after an assurance from the church there that she had been 'baptized and come under hands'. Three days after their marriage he was elected co-elder with Jameson and the Berkhamstead congregation sent over an elder who joined Jameson in laying hands on Bennet to 'ordain him an elder or overseer of this congregation'.

But in April 1679 the meetinghouse was still not paid for and the two deacons were asked to approach for their help all those who had not yet contributed: as late as June 1681 the matter was not settled and the deacons were asked to approach the non-contributors again. After a decision in January 1680 reaffirming their original determination not to invite preachers unless they were committed to the Six Principles, information about the life of the church grows sparse except for a continuing list of burials. Whether this was because persecution grew hotter or because it was decided to limit the records in any case cannot now be determined.

The Popish Plot and the Exclusionist Crisis

That the sporadic persecution in the 1670s, even after the easing signalled by the Declaration of Indulgence and the uncertainties which followed, had its effects cannot be doubted as has been seen in Bristol. In Reading, Berkshire, in 1674 a former member of the General Baptist church there who had become a Quaker, James Luddington, wrote, in the course of a debate with his former fellow-churchmembers, 'unless there be a very late increase they need not fear the late act against conventicles'.[39] The implication of this acid gibe that the General Baptist leader there, Daniel Roberts and his family, could not muster more than five additional adults for their meetings need not be taken entirely literally for it to be recognised, nonetheless, that their numbers had been cruelly affected by the persecution.

However, in the period 1678-1681 the scare connected with the Popish Plot and the parliamentary Exclusionist crisis took some of the heat of persecution from Protestant Dissenters generally if only to add to the misfortunes of the English Roman Catholic community. The most famous propagandist, if not the architect, of the Popish Plot was the scoundrel Titus Oates. He was the son of the Baptist evangelist Samuel Oates of the Cromwellian period and some were happy enough to fasten upon this link with the Baptists though they on their part hastened, with justice, utterly to disown him. The essence of the claims made by Oates and other informers was that a group of Roman Catholics had been planning to murder the king to put his brother, the Duke of York who had become a convert to Roman Catholicism, on his throne. This would, of course, be only a prelude to the forcible conversion of the whole kingdom to Rome. The difficulty then and now is to know whether there was any real fire beneath the smoke. It was an age of plots and counterplots, an age of uncertainty and of constitutional insecurity. Whatever the truth of the matter many, perhaps most, Englishmen, believed it and the government gave way to popular hysteria by executing some of the alleged plotters.

Meanwhile James, Duke of York, remained heir to the throne and a movement gathered force to deny him the succession. In March 1679 the House of Commons passed a bill to exclude James from the succession, and to prevent it becoming law the king dissolved parliament. The new parliament, reluctantly summoned by the king in October 1680, saw another attempt to exclude James. A new exclusionist bill passed the Commons but was rejected in the Lords who were influenced by the king. The king then dissolved the second exclusionist parliament in January 1681 and summoned a third to meet in royalist Oxford safely protected from the protestant enthusiasms of the London mob, in March 1681. While the House of Commons prepared yet another exclusionist bill the king announced another dissolution having secured the financial assistance he needed from Louis XIV. Parliament was not to meet again during his lifetime and he did not now need the money which only parliamentary taxes had previously provided.

There were two political consequences of this period. First, the king who had previously tended to have some sympathy with the Dissenters, now moved against them because they had strongly supported the Anglicans in the Exclusionist agitation. At the same time moderate Anglicans began to seek the support of the Dissenters as their own fears of the consequences of a Roman Catholic succession mounted. Nevertheless, while this was so at one level, the political, at the same time there were sufficient zealous churchmen anxious to carry through the policy of persecution which now had the royal support. As G R Cragg wrote of the Dissenters' experience after 1681, "never had their sufferings been so bitter or so prolonged".[40] The effects were widespread and were to have a lasting effect into the period of Toleration and well into the Eighteenth Century: 'Persecution, social pressure and the inducements of advantage were steadily depriving the Nonconformists of their rich and prominent members'.[41]

The General Baptist, Francis Smith, whose news-sheet *Smith's Protestant Intelligence* had played a considerable part in the 1681 Exclusionists' election campaign, was committed to Newgate on a charge of treason. He had for many years been the leading publisher for his denomination and had printed a number of devotional works including one of his own entitled *Symtomes of growth and decay in godlines* (1660, reprinted 1672, 1673). However a series f prosecutions, fines and imprisonments during the 1680s finally ruined him. In 1689 the White's Alley Churchbook recorded a grant of ten shillings to him 'considering his necessitous condition'. In 1683 he had shared in the fight to protect the charter of the City of London against the king's determination to remodel it as he was in the process of doing for many provincial towns to ensure that dissenters were kept out and royalists were kept in power.[42]

Some time earlier, on 2 October 1675, the London Calvinistic Baptist leaders had sent a circular letter to the churches in communion with them in England and Wales to invite representatives to meet with them in the capital the following May. Their intention, they said, was to form a plan for providing a regular and scholarly ministry for their churches 'who might give themselves to reading and study'.[43] Among the signatories were Daniel Dyke, William Collins and William Kiffin. Whether the meeting was ever actually held is unknown but it is clear that concern for the next generation of ministers was likely to become acute during the next few years as the few men who had received a university education grew old and the English universities continued closed to them. By this time a large number of those who had given leadership to the Calvinistic Baptists in the 1650s were dead: Thomas Patient, Kiffin's co-pastor, had died in 1666, Thomas Glasse in the same year, John Wigan in 1665, John Vernon in 1667, Abraham Cheare and possibly John Spilsbury in 1668 and Edward Harrison by March 1674. This meant that Kiffin and Hanserd Knollys were by that time the chief links with the age of the 1640s which had seen their denomination's first foundation. No doubt Knollys with his own publications on the subject would be one of those who in 1689 would press that young ministers should have a grasp of the languages in which the Scriptures were originally written.

Both men had known their share of troubles during the Persecution time. Knollys had been one of those incarcerated in Newgate gaol in consequence of the Venner rising right at the beginning of it all but had shared in the general pardon issued to mark the coronation. For a while afterwards he went into self-imposed exile in Holland and Germany with his family. He was back in London by 1666 to share with Edward Harrison in setting Thomas Patient apart as co-pastor with William Kiffin but was sent to prison again as the result of the Second Conventicle Act though he was apparently freed in time to marry Benjamin Keach (probably by then a recruit from the General Baptists) to his second wife in April 1672. He was in prison for another six months during 1684 and during that time was questioned, on behalf of the king, as to whether he and the Calvinistic Baptist community would accept a royal gesture of toleration. Knollys who was then in his middle eighties said that he was old and knew few men's minds. However being pressed further he said, 'I am of opinion that no liberty but what came by act of parliament would be acceptable because that would be stable, firm and certain'.[44] Undoubtedly this conviction would be widespread throughout Dissent.

William Kiffin's position as a wealthy London merchant undoubtedly gave him a security and a standing which even Hanserd Knollys, dependent upon an income from writing, from teaching and his pastorate, had not. Kiffin was able to intercede successfully for his co-religionists with the king, to make a gift of £10,000 to that monarch, and to become master of the company of Leathersellers as well as lead an illegal congregation throughout the persecution. He was to be involved with nearly every important decision and as a signatory of nearly every important document, including the Confessions of 1644 and 1677/89, during a long life of leadership among the Calvinistic Baptists and there is evidence that he was trusted in spite of (or perhaps because of?) his strict-communion views among the Arminians and the Seventh Day Baptists too. But all this could not save his grandsons when they were caught after the Monmouth rising even when Judge Jeffreys or one of his underlings was offered £3,000 for them. Nor could it keep Kiffin himself out of prison twice during the Persecution time.[45]

During the easement given by the excitements of the Popish Plot at least one group of churches began to attempt association meetings once more. The nucleus of this company seems to have been provided by the Petty France Church in London and a number of those congregations which in the days of the Protectorate had been part of the Abingdon Association. Possibly this had developed from the initiative over ministerial training in 1675 and the agreement over the Confession in 1677. At all events the first meeting took place at Hemel Hempstead, Hertfordshire, 2 April 1678.

Nehemiah Coxe, son of the Benjamin Coxe who had been active in that association during the earlier days and pastor with William Collins at Petty France, attended the meeting. On his return he gave an encouraging report of the proceedings of 'the messengers of the associated churches' and of their desire that 'for the future some brethren on behalf of this and other congregations in the city' should share in the meetings. Whether there was a larger London participation as a result is unknown, but, after the second meeting, held at Abingdon, Berkshire in September 1678 and the two 1679 meetings in London in March 1679 and at Hempstead in September thereafter the gatherings were held annually - at St Albans, Hertfordshire in March 1680; at Abingdon in April 1681, at Hempstead in April 1682 and in London, in April 1683.[46]

The Renewal of Persecution

Meanwhile the persecution grew hot once more. One professional informer claimed in 1682 to be employing fifty men to track down conventicles every Sunday. His work had been so successful that during the previous six months those whom he had been responsible for discovering and convicting had paid, in the city of London, £10,000 and in Westminster, £7,000 in fines.[47] It has been suggested that decent people were disgusted by the activities of informers. No doubt they were and in rural, closeknit communities, public opinion might well discourage those plying this unlovely trade. But in bigger, more urban, circumstances such scorn might well be less likely to bite and in the enormous sprawl of London the informers could be largely anonymous and so be protected from the censure of neighbours. From the authorities' point of view the informers certainly added a measure of efficiency to the working of the Second Conventicle Act by forcing even unwilling and good-natured local officials to obey it. At the same time it has also been suggested that the new scientific sceptical thought world into which England was now moving would almost certainly make toleration shortly inevitable. With the erosion of old certainties there would be less willingness to persecute over points of doctrine and no doubt less willingness stubbornly to hold to them under pressure. While this was doubtless true in the long run the harshness of the persecution of Dissent and of the Baptists in 1681-86 must be put down to more than royal policy.

Anglican treatment of Dissent over the thirty-five years down to the accession of George I (and even for several generations after that) was that of a body, even while growing less concerned for unanimity over doctrinal detail, which was consistently concerned for its own monopoly of all the political power it could preserve. In addition to this, no doubt, there was the sense that Dissent had been responsible for republican revolution and that society could only be safe if there were one church in the land to give the country its cement of faith, worship and discipline. The zeal with which bishops pursued Dissent down to the Revolution; the grudging measure of toleration granted to Dissent afterwards in spite of many hopes fostered by those whom D R Lacey called 'moderate' Anglicans; and the efforts by both mobs and churchmen, down to the death of Queen Anne, to erode that toleration together with the unwillingness of politicians throughout the eighteenth century to restore the full rights of citizenship to Dissenters suggest that the idea of equal toleration was far from being an Anglican ideal for many decades.

While the sufferings, the additional sufferings, of Dissent in the early and middle 1680s were in part the consequence of royal policy, there can be no doubt that the policy was carried through with a zeal and faithfulness by many churchmen which could not easily be forgotten by those who suffered it. The editor of the letters from parish clergy of the diocese of Oxford reporting on the Dissenters in their districts to Bishop Fell in 1682-83 has fairly commented on entrenched attitudes on both sides but also makes the point[48] that the clergy automatically looked to the magistracy to suppress the conventicles which nurtured and maintained nonconformity. It was, after all, the law.

The Rye House Plot was, like so much in this age of plotting, a very muddled affair. The government was given information about it by one Josiah Keeling (himself thought to be a Baptist) in June 1683. It is not clear how many of the Whig radicals who had been defeated in their attempts to exclude James II from the succession were involved. Certainly not all were Dissenters though one of the leaders, John Hampden, was a committed Presbyterian and several Baptists were linked with it including Thomas Walcott, a former Cromwellian officer, who was to be responsible for the attack on the king's guards as they passed the Rye House which was owned by another Baptist, Richard Rumbold. Abraham Holmes was another former Cromwellian officer and a Baptist who was involved with the affair and was to share in

Monmouth's rising a couple of years later. The government was glad to be able to tar all its opposition with the brush of rebellion and a great fuss was made in order to involve as many of the Whigs as possible while laying most of the blame for the whole on the Dissenters generally. The Baptists' earlier history helped to encourage the beliefs of those who wished to see them all as by nature revolutionaries and who refused to see any explanation for their acts in the desperation to which they were driven.[49]

James II and the Revolution of 1688

When Charles II was succeeded by his brother, an avowed Roman Catholic, on 6 February 1685, many Dissenters reached a point of desperation. Their situation which had already been serious could now, they believed, become hopeless.

As a result there was considerable support that June among many Dissenters throughout the country in words, and in parts of the west country in deeds for the ill-conceived attempt by the Duke of Monmouth, illegitimate son of Charles II, to capture the throne. A number of Baptists were involved among the rebels. One was Sampson Larke, the Calvinistic Baptist pastor at Lyme. He had played a part among the London churches during the Interregnum and had spent ten years in Exeter gaol for refusing an oath of loyalty to the new king in 1661. After the failure of the rising he was executed at Lyme. Others, like Abraham Holmes who had been one of Cromwell's officers and who had also been in prison at least once since the restoration, and the two grandsons of William Kiffin, Benjamin and William Hewling, were also executed. Some were more fortunate. Andrew Gifford, pastor at the Pithay in Bristol, who had hoped to encourage Monmouth to take the city had gathered considerable money and ammunition for his support. Monmouth and his forces turned away and Gifford's part did not become known until years afterwards. Henry Danvers, who had been in and out of trouble for many years since becoming a Baptist while governor of Stafford during the civil war, fled to Holland when the rising failed. He had opposed Cromwell's being Lord Protector, he had been a Fifth Monarchist, had been gaoled for a while after the restoration and had then plotted support for Monmouth in London. He died a year or so later still an exile. The consequences of the rising were extremely serious for the Dissenters for, as D R Lacey wrote, never 'had the Court and Anglican leaders had such a convincing reason for stringent persecution as after the Monmouth Rebellion, and never had the Nonconformists greater reason to feel that it was hopeless to expect relief than they did following the Bloody Assizes'.[50]

However, help was very soon to be given even though from an utterly unexpected source. In the spring of 1686 the new king himself reversed his earlier policy and turned from supporting the Church of England towards easing the lot of the Dissenters. On 10 March he issued a general pardon freeing from gaol all those of his subjects who had been imprisoned on grounds of religion. Meanwhile, although the Anglicans continued to harry the Dissenters, the change in the wind was made clear by such experiences as those of Henry Forty and the Abingdon Baptists. In July 1686 Henry Forty, who had previously served in the west country and as a successor to Henry Jessey in London, was now pastor at Abingdon. He and a number of his co-defendants were freed from the prosection they were enduring under the earlier laws and were released on Saturday 10 July. At once they set about preparing and cleaning their meeting house, which had been shut up because of the persecution, for worship. Next day hundreds came to the morning and afternoon services.[51]

In November the king's protection was made more generally effective through the establishment of a Licence

Office. There, for fifty shillings, a licence could be purchased to protect a whole family from all legal proceedings for their nonconformity.[52]

The king's attempts to win the support of the Dissenters continued with his issue, on 4 April 1687, of his first Declaration of Indulgence. Naturally the Court at once began to press the nonconforming communities to respond with expressions of their gratitude. To do this, however, presented immediate difficulties: to present addresses of gratitude was to condone, or at least to appear to condone, James II's use of the royal prerogative. William Kiffin and Joseph Stennett, the learned Seventh Day Baptist Leader, opposed any form of address at all, as did Richard Baxter and other leaders among the Presbyterians and Independents. The addresses which did come in did not apparently, _in any case_, include statements approving the king's claim to power to dispense any of his subjects from the effects of the laws of the land. A number explicitly expressed the hope that the declaration would ultimately be supported with a parliamentary decision. Against advice an address of gratitude was submitted by a group of ministers led by Nehemiah Cox from the London Calvinistic Baptists. One of the signatories was also the minister of the Barbican church, Thomas Plant. The Barbican was a church which moved somewhat uneasily between the Calvinistic Baptists and the Generals before, ultimately, long outside the period of this chapter, settling for the Generals.[53]

Meanwhile many Anglicans were viewing the king's policies towards his Roman Catholic co-religionists with growing alarm and it was during this period that informal but serious promises were beginning to be made to Dissenting leaders by a number of Anglican leaders as they sought the support of the Dissenters against popery. It was the way in which these promises were forgotten after the revolution that caused a great deal of Dissenting bitterness. However, not all Anglicans were afraid of Rome. In April, Thomas White, bishop of Peterborough, was quite dogmatically insisting that there was 'no danger at all of Popery, but only of the fanatics'. As the situation developed the Dissenters were certainly placed in a difficult position: they had reason to fear an alliance both on the one side with the Court and the Roman Catholics and, on the other, with the Anglicans though their leaders, especially among the Presbyterians, now moved towards close political co-operation with the moderate Anglicans. Meanwhile there was considerable public debate about the intentions of William of Orange. Court propaganda was naturally inclined to play down his potential support for Dissent whilst his allies in England, of course, tended to emphasize it. By the spring of 1688 it seems fairly clear the king's new policy had failed to win the Presbyterians, the most numerous and influential wing of Dissent.[54]

From the king's point of view the Second Declaration of Indulgence, 27 April 1688, made things worse. While it insisted that he would now work for a toleration established by law and otherwise contained the same substance as before the Anglican clergy were required to read it from their pulpits. In their refusal to do this they sought and found Dissenting support because to do so would again, in effect, support his dispensing power. Not only did the Nonconformists in their turn refuse to read the Indulgence to their people and to return thanks for it: their alarm, like that of many of their fellow Protestants, was further increased by the birth, 10 July 1688, of a Roman Catholic heir to the throne. The Orange succession looked as if it might be postponed for good. Now Dissenters became aware of the irony that they, branded by their Anglican neighbours for a generation and more as revolutionaries, saw those same neighbours supporting a group of potential rebels who invited William of Orange to invade their country and take their throne! But William's landing in Torbay on 5 November and the subsequent flight of the king were entirely welcome to Dissenters nonetheless. William Kiffin himself led a deputation of Baptists to present an address of welcome to the new rulers of England on 2 January 1689 and made a personal contribution of £500 towards the financial needs of William's government when it sought to raise a loan to tide itself over the first six months.[55]

The Toleration Act, as it came to be known, which was eventually passed by the new government, 'gave, as may be supposed from the temper of the times, the smallest possible advantage to Dissenters from the established religion'. Yet, while Skeats and Miall were justified in this rather sour judgement, it was to provide a solid constitutional basis for the protection of Dissenters in days to come, even with its rather negative title, 'An act for exempting their Majesties' Protestant subjects dissenting from the Church of England from the penalties of certain laws'. Admittedly toleration was only extended to Trinitarian Protestants; admittedly their ministers had to subscribe to thirty-six out of the Thirty Nine Articles (Baptists were further excused subscription to that referring to infant baptism), admittedly they must still pay tithes and church rates to the established church, admittedly the sacramental test for public office still remained, admittedly their meeting places must be licensed and would only be on condition that the oaths of supremacy and allegiance were taken, but, nonetheless, the Act was greeted with a sigh of relief by the Baptists as much as their fellow Dissenters.[56]

The two Baptist groupings - they could almost be described as denominations now - took the opportunity, as soon as was possible, to put their mutual houses in order. The General Baptists were the first to arrange to summon a national assembly, 21 May 1689. The records of the meeting show little sign of their being aware that a new day had dawned. However, the London Calvinistic Baptist leaders wrote to their brethren throughout the country on 22 July inviting them to send delegates to meet in the capital 'with the rest of the elders and brethren of the churches in London' on 3 September. Their letter not only spoke of their gratitude for their recent deliverance but expressed concern at the state of the churches and the ministry. The churches were asked to reply either to Hanserd Knollys or to William Kiffin. These were elder statesmen indeed: Knollys was on the eve of his ninetieth birthday and Kiffin was seventy-three. They were among the very few who had led in the golden days of the 1640s and 1650s who still remained. Soon they would be gone and, as the century drew to its close, the bright hopes of 1689 would begin to grow dull.[57]

An interesting account but some sociological analysis would be interesting.

NOTES AND REFERENCES

Abbreviations used

A.R.P.B.	B. R. White (ed), *Association Records of the Particular Baptists of England, Wales and Ireland to 1660*, 3 vols. and index, Baptist Historical Society, 1971-77.
B.Q.	*Baptist Quarterly*
Crosby I,II,III,IV	Thomas Crosby, *Gangraena*, 1646 (Facsimile edited by M. M. Goldsmith and Ivan Roots, the Rota Press, Exeter 1977).
Ivimey I,II,III,IV	Joseph Ivimey, *History of the English Baptists*, 4 vols., 1811-30.
Lumpkin	W. L. Lumpkin, *Baptist Confessions of Faith*, Chicago 1959.
M.G.A. I,II	W. T. Whitley (ed.)*Minutes of the General Assembly of General Baptists*, 2 vols., 1909-10.
R.C.C.	E. B. Underhill, *Records of the Churches of Christ gathered at Fenstanton, Warboys and Hexham 1644-1720*, 1854.
T.B.H.S.	*Transactions of the Baptist Historical Society*

Where no place of publication is given, London should be assumed.

The spelling of the quotations has been modernised.

Chapter 1. The English General Baptists to 1660

1 Champlin Burrage, *The Early English Dissenters*, 2 vols., Cambridge, 1912, 41-67.

2 B. R. White, *The English Separatist Tradition*, 1971, *passim*.

3 *B.Q.*, XVI, 303-12.

4 *Ibid.*, 339-42.

5 Lonnie D. Kliever, 'General Baptist Origins: the question of Anabaptist Influence', and Glen H. Stassen, 'Anabaptist Influence in the Origin of the Particular Baptists', *Mennonite Quarterly Review*, XXXVI, 1962, 291-348.

6 John Robinson, *Of Religious Communion*, Leyden, 1614, 48.

7 Richard Clifton, *A Plea for Infants*, Amsterdam, 1610, 'An answer to Mr Smyth's Epistle to the Reader'.

8 John Smyth, *Works*, II, (ed. Whitley) Cambridge 1950,757.

9 Champlin Burrage, *op.cit.*, II, 185.

10 *Lumpkin*, 116-23.

11 B. Evans, *Early English Baptists*, 2 vols., 1864, II, 21-44. Cf., Champlin Burrage, *op.cit.*, II, 222-257.

12 *Gangraena*, I, 92-5.

13 *Crosby*, III, 55.

14 E. Barber, *To the Kings Most Excellent Majesty*, 1641.

15 E. Barber, *A small Treatise of Baptisme or Dipping*, 1642, 11 f.

16 E. Barber, *The humble Request of certaine Christians*, 1643.

17 H. Danvers, *A Treatise of Laying on of Hands*, 1674, 58.

18 *Crosby*, III, 97-9; W. Jeffery, *The Whole Faith of Man*, 2nd edn. 1659, 60-4.

19 E. Barber, *A true Discovery of the Ministery of the Gospel*, 1645, 1-14.

20 E. Barber, *An Answere to the Essex Watchmens Watchword*, 1649, 1, 10, 16.

21 *Gangraena*, II, 146-8, III, 105 f, 189.

22 A. Betteridge, 'Early Baptists in Leicestershire and Rutland', *B.Q.*, XXV, 206-10.

23 *Crosby*, III, 61.

24 *Gangraena*, I, 76 f, 181 f, III, 86 f.

25 J. Drew, *A Serious Addresse to Samuel Oates*, 1649, 14 margin.

26 *R.C.C.*, 1-264.

27 *Ibid.*, 267 ff.

28 *Lumpkin*, 174-88; John Griffiths, *Gods Oracle and Christs Doctrine*, 1655, 61.

29 *R.C.C.*, 60-8, 69, 71, 127-30, 143, 202-6.

30 *M.G.A.*, I, 1-5, 6-9.

31 *R.C.C.*, 71-3, 83 f, 101 f, 105-8, 109, 111-13, 114, 134 f.

32 *Crosby*, I, 306 f.

33 *R.C.C.*, 5 f, 21, 33, 41, 49, 115.

34 *Ibid.*, 36 f, 69 f, 135-7.

35 *Ibid.*, 16-19, 167 f, 221-3, 238-40.

36 *Ibid.*, 103-5, 108 f.

37 M. Spufford, *Contrasting Communities*, 1974, 346 f. See *R.C.C.* 19, 82 f, 244 f, 110 f, 207, 210 f.

38 *R.C.C.*, 72. William Jeffery, *op.cit.*, 95-100.

39 *R.C.C.*, 155-7, 195, 188 f, 144-6, 98, 124 f, 187, 200.

40 *Ibid.*, 195-8, 204 f.

41 *Ibid.*, 36 f, 108 f, 126 f, 140 f, 144, 147, 155 f.

42 John Griffith, *A Treatise touching falling from Grace*, 1653, Preface 'To all the elders and deacons ... in the county of Kent'.

43 *T.B.H.S.*, III, 1912-13, 247-50.

44 *M.G.A.*, I, 1-22.

45 G. E. Aylmer, *The Levellers in the English Revolution*, 1975, 11.

46 *Gangraena*, III, 30 f, *Crosby*, IV, 248 f, D. M. Wolfe, *Leveller Manifestoes of the Puritan Revolution*, 1967, 237-41.

47 W. Haller and C. Davies, *The Leveller Tracts 1647-53*, 1964, (Gloucester, Massachusetts), 355 f, 374. Murray Tolmie, 'Thomas Lambe, soapboiler, and Thomas Lambe, merchant, General Baptists', *B.Q.* XXVII, 1977-78, and E. Barber, *An answer, op.cit.*, 8-10.

48 *M.G.A.*, I, 2-5, 6. *Lumpkin*, 194, 230, 232 f.

49 E. B. Underhill, *Confessions of Faith*, 1854, 343-52, 353-6, 357-60.

Chapter 2. The Calvinistic Baptists to 1660

1 B. R. White, 'The doctrine of the Church in the Particular Baptist Confession of 1644', *Journal of Theological Studies*, N.S., vol.XIX, 1968, 570-90.

2 *Ibid.*, 574-5.

3 Both the 1596 and the 1644 Confessions are printed in *Lumpkin*, 82-97, 156-171.

4 R. G. Torbet, *A History of the Baptists*, Rev. edn. 1963, 44.

5 *A.R.P.B.*, 114 (the Irish letter) and 9 (the Welsh response).

6 *Ibid.*, 126-9.

7 *D.N.B.* and B. R. White, 'William Kiffin - Baptist Pioneer and Citizen of London', *Baptist History and Heritage*, vol.2, 91-103.

8 B. R. White, 'Thomas Patient in England and Ireland', *Irish Baptist Historical Society Journal*, vol.2, 36-48.

9 W. T. Whitley, 'The Reverend Colonel Paul Hobson, Fellow of Eton', *B.Q.*, IX, 307-10.

10 B. R. White, *Hanserd Knollys and Radical Dissent in the 17th Century*, 1977.

11 B. R. White, 'Henry Jessey, a Pastor in Politics', *B.Q.*, XXV, 98-110 and 'Henry Jessey in the Great Rebellion', *Reformation, Conformity and Dissent*, edited by R. Buick Knox, 1977, 132-53.

12 *D.N.B.* entry is extensive but requires bringing up to date.

13 B. Coxe, *An appendix to a Confession of Faith*, 1646 in *Confessions of Faith* edited by E. B. Underhill, 1854.

14 *A.R.P.B.*, 103, 109 note 51.

15 *Confessions of Faith, op.cit.*, 275, 280, 282, 284.

16 *Ibid.*, 289 f.

17 B. R. White, 'John Miles and the structures of the Calvinistic Baptist mission to South Wales 1649-1660', *Welsh Baptist Studies* edited by M. John, 1976, 35-76.

18 *Confessions of Faith, op.cit.* 294 f, 305, 308 f.

19 *A.R.P.B.*, 111-24.

20 *Ibid.*, 131.

21 W. T. Whitley, 'Benjamin Coxe', *T.B.H.S.*, 6, 50-9.

22 *A.R.P.B.*, 135 f.

23 *Ibid.*, 43-50.

24 B. R. White, 'John Pendarves, the Calvinistic Baptists and the Fifth Monarchy', *B.Q.*, XXV, 251-271.

25 T. C. Barnard, *Cromwellian Ireland*, 1975, esp. 98-109.

26 *Confessions of Faith, op.cit.*, 335-8.

27 *A.R.P.B.*, 96-8.

28 *Ibid.*, 30.

29 *Ibid.*, 23, 151 f, 153-7, 62 f, 64, 69, Leominster Churchbook MS pp.148 f.

30 *A.R.P.B.*, 78.

31 *Ibid.*, 98-101, 203-6.

Chapter 3. The Era of the Great Persecution 1660-1688

1 Clarendon, *History of the Rebellion and Civil Wars in England* (edited by W. D. Macray) 1888, VI, 206 f.

2 R. A. Beddard, 'The Restoration Church', *The Restored Monarchy 1660-1688* (edited by J. R. Jones) 1979, 155.

3 Jessey, H., *The Lords Loud Call to England*, 1660, 8, 13, 15 ff, 24 ff.

4 E. B. Underhill (ed), *Tracts on Liberty of Conscience*, 1846, 313.

5 *Lumpkin*, 220-235; *Confessions of Faith*, 343-352.

6 Adis, H., *A fanaticks Addresse*, 1661, 4, 5, 15 f.

7 J. P. Kenyon, *The Stuart Constitution 1603-1688*, 1969, 376-8.

8 *A narrative of the ... execution of John James*, Anon., 1662, 7, 9, 12.

9 J. Walker, 'The Yorkshire Plot 1663', *Yorkshire Archaeological Journal*, XXXI, 1932-4, 348-59 and B. S. Capp, *The Fifth Monarchy Men*, 1972.

10 D. Ogg, *England in the Reign of Charles II*, 2nd edn. 1956, I, 200-1.

11 J. P. Kenyon, *op.cit.*, 378-82.

12 Cf. references in A. G. Matthews, *Calamy Revised*, 1934.

13 *Ibid.*, xi-xiii.

14 E. A. Payne and N. S. Moon, *Baptists and 1662*, 1962, 12 f.

15 A. E. Preston, *St Nicholas, Abingdon and other papers*, 1935, 118 f.

16 R. Hayden (ed), *Broadmead Records*, Bristol Records Society vol.XXVII, 1974, 117 f.

17 J. E. Neale, *Elizabeth and her Parliaments 1584-1601*, 1957, 286-94.

18 *Ivimey*, I, 335-8.

19 J. P. Kenyon, *op.cit.*, 383-6.

20 *Ibid.*, 384 note 1.

21 A. E. Preston, *op.cit.*, 122-6.

22 *R.C.C.*, 278; *M.G.A.*, I, 23.

23 W. T. Whitley, *Baptist Bibliography*, 1916, vol.I.

24 G. R. Cragg, *Puritanism in the Age of the Great Persecution*, 1957, 13 f.

25 J. P. Kenyon, *op.cit.*, 383-6.

26 G. R. Cragg, *op.cit.*, 17.

27 R. Hayden, *op.cit.*, 134, 136.

28 J. R. Jones, *Country and Court: England 1658-1714*, 1978, 176.

29 R. Hayden, *op.cit.*, 144-6.

30 *Ibid.*, 225.

31 *Ibid.*, 149 f, 161, 163, 171, 180.

32 *Ibid.*, 185 f, 209.

33 R. L. Greaves and R. Zaller, *Biographical Dictionary of British Radicals in the Seventeenth Century*, 1982, I, 139.

34 A. Cheare, *Words in Season*, 1668, 252, 248, 254, 263 ff.

35 T. Grantham, *Christianismus Primitivus*, 1678, 11, 121-3, 126, 130, 139, 141.

36 *Lumpkin*, 287-9.

37 *Ibid.*, 317-20, 327.

38 W. T. Whitley (ed), *The Church Books of Ford or Cuddington and Amersham*, 1912, 201-229.

39 B. R. White, 'The Baptists of Reading 1652-1715', *B.Q.*, XXII, 1967-8, 259.

40 G. R. Cragg, *op.cit.*, 26.

41 *Ibid.*, 193.

42 D. R. Lacey, *Dissent and Parliamentary Politics in England 1661-89*, 1969, 115 f, 155.

43 *Ivimey*, I, 417.

44 *Ibid.*, 420.

45 B. R. White, 'William Kiffin, Baptist Pioneer and Citizen of London', *Baptist History and Heritage*, vol.II, 1967.

46 *Ivimey*, III, 333.

47 M. R. Watts, *The Dissenters from the Reformation to the French Revolution*, 1978, 254.

48 M. Clapinson (ed), *Bishop Fell and Nonconformity*, Oxford Record Society, 1980, xxxvii.

49 M. R. Watts, *op.cit.*, 256.

50 D. R. Lacey, *op.cit.*, 174.

51 *Ibid.*, 176; *Ivimey*, I, 464.

52 D. R. Lacey, *op.cit.*, 179.

53 *Ibid.*, 180; *Ivimey*, I, 471 f.

54 D. R. Lacey, *op.cit.*, 187 ff.

55 *Ibid.*, 223, 357 note 55.

56 H. S. Skeats and C. S. Miall, *History of the Free Churches of England 1688-1891*, 1891, 104.

57 *M.G.A.*, I, 25-8; *Ivimey*, I, 478-80.

SELECT BIBLIOGRAPHY

W. H. Burgess — *John Smyth, the Se-Baptist.* 1911.

T. Crosby — *The History of the English Baptists.* 4 Vols. 1738-40.

B. Evans — *The Early English Baptists.* 2 Vols. 1864.

R. Hayden — *The Records of a Church of Christ in Bristol, 1640-87.* Bristol. 1974.

D. M. Himbury — *British Baptists: A Short History.* 1962.

J. Ivimey — *History of the Baptists.* 4 Vols. 1811-30.

W. L. Lumpkin — *Baptist Confessions of Faith.* Chicago. 1959.

E. A. Payne and N. S. Moon — *Baptists and 1662.* 1962.

E. A. Payne — *The Fellowship of Believers.* (1944). Rev.edn. 1952.

E. A. Payne — *The Baptist Union: A Short History.* 1959.

H. Wheeler Robinson — *The Life and Faith of the Baptists.* 1927.

H. S. Skeats and C. S. Miall — *The History of the Free Churches of England: 1688-1891.* 1891.

E. C. Starr — *Baptist Bibliography.* 25 Vols. Rochester, U.S.A.

A. Taylor — *A History of the English General Baptists.* 1818.

E. B. Underhill — *Confessions of Faith.* 1854.

E. B. Underhill — *Records of the Churches of Christ Gathered at Fenstanton, Hexham and Warboys: 1644-1720.* 1854.

R. C. Walton — *The Gathered Community.* 1946.

B. R. White — *The English Separatist Tradition.* 1971.

B. R. White — *Hanserd Knollys and Radical Dissent in the Seventeenth Century.* 1977.

B. R. White — *Association Records of the Particular Baptists of England, Wales and Ireland to 1660.* 1977.

W. T. Whitley — *A History of the British Baptists.* (1923). Rev. edn. 1932.

W. T. Whitley — *The Baptists of London.* n.d.

W. T. Whitley *The Works of John Smyth.* 1915.

W. T. Whitley *Minutes of the General Assembly of General Baptists.* 2 vols. 1910.

W. T. Whitley *Baptist Bibliography.* 2 vols. 1916, 1922.

W. T. Whitley *The Church Books of Ford, Cuddington and Amersham.* 1912.

J. Wood *A Condensed History of the General Baptists of the New Connexion.* 1847.

SEVENTEENTH CENTURY WORKS CITED

Adis, H., *A fanaticks Addresse*, 143n.

Agreement of the People, 38,55.

Barber, E., *An Answere to the Essex Watchmens Watchword*, 140n-1.

The humble Request of certaine Christians, 140n.

A small Treatise of Baptisme or Dipping, 34, 140n.

To the kings most excellent majesty, 34,140n.

A true Discovery of the Ministery of the Gospel, 35-6,140n.

Broadmead Records, 9 (R. Hayden, ed.) 144n.

(E. B. Underhill, ed.) 19.

Cheare, A., *Words in Season*, 113,144n.

Clarendon, *History of the Rebellion and Civil Wars in England*, 143n.

Clifton, R., *A Plea for infants*, 140n.

Cotton, J., *The keyes of the kingdom of heaven*, 66.

Cox, B., *An appendix to a confession of faith*, 72.

Danvers, H., *A Treatise of Laying on of Hands*, 140n.

A Declaration of Faith (1611), 26.

Denne, H., *The Levellers designe discovered*, 40.

A description of what God hath predestinated (1620), 28.

Drew, J., *A Serious Address to Samuel Oates*, 141n.

Edwards, T., *Gangraena*, 32,74,140n-1.

An essay toward settlement upon a sure foundation, 86.

The faith and practice of thirty congregations, 41-2,51.

Grantham, T., *Christianismus Primitivus*, 114-6.

Griffiths, J., *Gods Oracle and Christs Doctrine*, 44,141n.

A Treatise touching falling from Grace, 141n.

Haller, W. and Davies, C., *The Leveller Tracts*, 141n.

Heartbleedings for professors abominations, 78,80.

Helwys, T., *A Short Declaration of the Mystery of Iniquity*, 27.

The humble apology, 45,56.

The humble representation and vindication, 43,54,56-7.

Jeffery, W., *The Whole Faith of Man*, 44,140n.

Jessey, H. *The Lord's Loud Call to England*, 94,143n.

Jessey, Kiffin and others, *A Declaration*, 74.

Lumpkin, W. L., *Baptist Confessions of Faith*, 140n-3.

A narrative of the ... execution of John James, 143n.

Objections argued by way of dialogue ... that no man ought to be persecuted for his religion, 28.

Robinson, J., *Of Religious Communion*, 140n.

The second humble address, 56.

The second part of England's new chains discovered, 75.

Smith, F., *Symtomes of growth and decay in godliness*, 127.

Smith's Protestant intelligence, 127.

Spilsbury, J., *A treatise concerning the lawful subject of baptisms*, 71.

Underhill, E. B., *Confessions of Faith*, 141n-3.

Records of the Churches of Christ, gathered at Fenstanton, Warboys, and Hexham, 19,41,49,141n,144n.

Tracts on Liberty of Conscience, 143n.

White, B. R. (ed.), *Association Records of the Particular Baptists of England, Wales and Ireland to 1660*, 142n-3.

Whitley, W. T. (ed.), *The Church Books of Ford or Cuddington and Amersham*, 19,144n.

Minutes of the General Assembly of the General Baptists,19,141n,144n-5.

Works of John Smyth, 19,140n.

Wolfe, D. M., *Leveller Manifestoes of the Puritan Revolution*, 141n.

INDEX